no cook

COOKBOOK

whitecap

over 200 simple
recipes and ideas
for mouthwatering
meals without cooking

no cook
COOKBOOK

orlando murrin

photography by jason lowe

to Peter

Editorial director: **Jane O'Shea** Art director: **Mary Evans**

Editor & project manager: **Lewis Esson** American editor: **Beverly Le Blanc**

Photography: **Jason Lowe** Home economist: **Jane Suthering**

Production: **Beverley Richardson**

First published in 2003 by Quadrille Publishing Limited,
Alhambra House, 27-31 Charing Cross Road, London WC2H OLS

Published in the US and Canada in 2003 by Whitecap Books
For more information, please contact Whitecap Books, 351 Lynn
Avenue, North Vancouver, British Columbia, Canada V7J 2C4

Text © Orlando Murrin 2003 Photography © Jason Lowe 2003
Design & layout © Quadrille Publishing Ltd 2003

The rights of Orlando Murrin to be identified as the Author of this
Work have been asserted by him in accordance with the Copyright,
Design and Patents Act 1988.

Cataloguing in Publication Data: a catalogue record for this book is
available from the British Library

ISBN 1-55285-534-1

Printed in China through World Print Ltd

no-cooking is easy... you don't need any specialist equipment and you don't have to master difficult techniques. It's all a question of choosing the best-quality ingredients and treating them sympathetically

no-cook guidelines

To get off to a good start, overleaf you'll find some helpful lists of those ingredients that I really find are a boon to the no-cook. At the end of the book (page 158), you'll also find a comprehensive list of those things that I recommend you keep in your cupboards to help make no-cooking even easier. Generally, these are the items I list in the recipe ingredients under the heading "Make sure you've got." While "What you need" lists those items I think you are probably going to have to buy specifically for the recipes in question.

You will see that the three concessions to cooking I allow myself are boiling water and melting chocolate and butter.

Happy no-cooking!

no-cook refrigerator & freezer requisites

herbs as they magically brighten flavors and turn ordinary ingredients into something special. Fresh cilantro gives a hint of the exotic; basil and tarragon the Med; chives make dishes lip-lickingly tasty; parsley freshens.

tomatoes because they are luscious, juicy, and taste of the sun. I usually halve them and squeeze out the pulp and seeds, as this makes them sweeter and tastier. Always choose cherry or vine-ripened tomatoes.

lemons and limes as they add a fresh, piquant note. Use grated lemon zest to give a zing. Go easy on the juice—it's often better to squeeze it over the finished dish than risk mixing it in. A flick of lime zest transports you instantly to the tropics.

cheeses because there's a different type for every occasion. Keep a supply of jars of goat cheese and feta in oil, bagged mozzarella for salads, hard cheeses for grating.

seafood as fresh shrimp, smoked salmon, and Avruga (herring) caviar spell instant luxury. Smoked salmon is a feast in itself, or can be conjured into snacks or salads.

green onions as they add instant pizzazz. I invariably shred them—trim, leaving a bit of green, then chop thinly at a sharp angle. Red onions add color.

celery and cucumber for their crunch. If you can find white celery, it tastes best, but always cut it finely. Cucumber can be used peeled or not. I usually first cut it down the middle and scoop out the pulpy seeds.

crème fraîche, fromage blanc and mascarpone as creams of every description are the no-cook's best friend, turning into instant silky sauces. Mascarpone is the most de luxe of all—beat it until just soft if it's too stiff.

cooked and smoked meats because they're convenient and usually very tasty. Try different flavors of cooked chickens—BBQ, Oriental, chargrilled—plus smoked chicken, turkey, duck, and venison, as well as hams—even crisp-fried bacon bits.

breads as the right bread establishes an instant atmosphere. Serve Italian breads with Mediterranean foods, pitas with Middle Eastern, rye with seafood and Scandinavian flavors, and turn tortillas into wraps, new-wave sandwiches.

arugula, watercress, and cress because they add a peppery bite. Use cress for sprinkling. Choose mixed bags of salad with care—they can contain too many types of leaf.

unsalted butter as salted butter might be fine for cooking and everyday use, but unsalted tastes cleaner and more refined, and can be used for sweet dishes as well as savory.

custard sauce because you can use it to whip up a quick dessert, and as a base for homemade ice cream and other glitzy desserts.

in the freezer

frozen peas and fava beans as they add a fresh, sweet note. Put in a bowl with a little salt, cover with boiling water, and leave for 10 minutes. Drain, cool quickly in cold water, and drain again.

ice cream because a tub of best-quality vanilla ice cream can be transformed in no time into a memorable dessert by stirring through extra ingredients such as chopped chocolate, nuts, marshmallows... you name it.

tortillas, breads, and muffins as they defrost in minutes for exciting hand-held lunches and suppers. Breads can be sliced from frozen and toasted into bruschettas and crostini; muffins crumbled for instant trifles.

shrimp because they can be used to make a quick feast.

5 great no-cook spices

crushed chilies Keep a small bowl on the table and you'll find you use them almost as much as black pepper. Good whenever you want a flavor lift.

cinnamon A warm, brown spice that goes beautifully with apples, pitted fruits, and Moroccan dishes. Try grinding cinnamon sticks in your coffee grinder for a marvelously deep, rich flavor and aroma.

poppy seeds Add crunch and a faint aniseed flavor to dishes with this delicate and pretty spice. Caraway seeds give a similar whiff of the exotic.

paprika Dust paprika over egg and vegetable dishes to give an appetizing appearance and a gently spiced first bite.

smoked paprika One of the boldest and most exciting flavors in the entire spice box. Use infrequently, in careful quantities, to give panache to chargrilled and spicy dishes.

On page 158 you'll also find a list of things I recommend you have in your cupboards to make no-cooking easier.

we live in an age of convenience meals
and take-outs—although these continue to get better
and better, for a little extra effort you can make far more creative
and exciting meals without the bother of cooking

instant suppers and lunches

crunchy duck and noodles

Serves 4 ● 15 to 20 minutes to prepare, keeps its crunch for 24 hours

Conjure this up when you're in the mood for something light but tasty—it's also good for a lunchbox. The best bit of the crunch comes from the water chestnuts, which squeak as you bite.

What you need

1 pound cooked duck, on the bone, or
   12 ounces off (Chinese restaurants sell
   cooked and BBQ duck—you'll need half
   a duck)

5 ounces fresh beansprouts

half a 7-ounce can of water chestnuts,
   drained, rinsed, and thinly sliced

2 green onions, shredded

1/2-inch cube of fresh root ginger, peeled and
   finely chopped

handful of fresh cilantro, chopped

Make sure you've got

instant Chinese noodles (5 ounces)

boiling water

1/2 red chili

hoisin sauce (2 tablespoons)

dry sherry (2 tablespoons)

dark sesame oil (2 teaspoons)

dark soy sauce (2 tablespoons)

1 orange

❶ Break the noodles into a pan or bowl and pour boiling water over them to cover generously; leave for 5 to 10 minutes.

❷ Meanwhile, discard the skin and bones from the duck and shred the meat (do this with your hands). Try and keep it in long, thin pieces.

❸ Mix the duck, beansprouts, chestnuts, green onions, ginger, and chili, seeded and finely chopped. Drain the noodles when ready and add these.

❹ Whisk the hoisin sauce, sherry, sesame oil, and soy sauce together and toss into the duck mixture (you probably won't need salt). Sprinkle the cilantro and orange juice over.

Drain the remaining water chestnuts, put them in a bowl and cover with water. They'll keep in the refrigerator for up to a week. Slice them thinly to use in salads and stir-fries.

make it your own You can use 3 celery stalks instead of the water chestnuts—slice them very thinly at an angle. ● You can also make this dish with cooked or barbecued chicken. Squeeze lemon juice over the finished dish instead of orange.

coconut-turkey noodles

Serves 4 ● 15 to 25 minutes to prepare

This makes a satisfying supper at relatively little cost, but is sufficiently intriguing in flavor to serve when entertaining guests.

What you need

14 ounces cooked turkey (or chicken or
    pork), preferably BBQ or chargrilled, cut
    into bite-size chunks

2 green onions, shredded

1 yellow, orange, or red bell pepper, seeded
    and thinly sliced

6 cherry tomatoes, halved or quartered

$2/3$ cup coconut cream

Make sure you've got

instant Chinese noodles (5 ounces)

boiling water

$1/2$ red chili, finely chopped

tomato catsup (2 teaspoons)

Worcestershire sauce

salt and pepper

❶ Put the noodles in a bowl, cover with boiling water, and leave for 5 to 10 minutes. Drain in a strainer or colander.

❷ While the noodles are soaking, put the turkey, green onions, chili, pepper, and tomatoes in a bowl. Pour the coconut cream, catsup, and a dash of Worcestershire sauce over. Add some seasoning and mix.

❸ Stir in the noodles to mix thoroughly, then divide among 4 plates.

make it your own **To give this dish a Hawaiian feel, sprinkle it with $1^1/2$ ounces chopped roasted macadamia nuts, which are indigenous to the islands, for a crunchy topping.**

tuna-artichoke pita breads (simple)

Makes 3 large pitas ● 10 to 20 minutes to make

What you need

3 large pitas, halved

7 tablespoons crème fraîche or sour cream

4 ounces artichokes in oil, drained and sliced

2 large tomatoes, halved, seeded, and sliced

small bunch of fresh mint, chopped

Make sure you've got

pesto (2 teaspoons)

canned tuna in oil (7 ounces)

pine nuts (2 tablespoons)

1 lemon

❶ If you like, warm the pita breads under the broiler or in a toaster.

❷ Mix the crème fraîche and pesto in a medium-size bowl. Pile in the drained and flaked tuna, the artichokes, the pine nuts, sliced tomatoes, and mint, and mix lightly.

❸ Spoon the filling into the pitas and squeeze some lemon juice over.

smoked turkey and mango wraps

Serves 4 (easily halved or quartered) ● 10 to 20 minutes to prepare

What you need

4 soft wheat tortillas, about 8 inches

7 ounces sliced smoked turkey or chicken

4-inch piece of cucumber, peeled, halved
    lengthwise, and sliced

2 handfuls of watercress, roughly chopped

1 ripe mango, peeled and cut into thick sticks

a few fresh basil leaves

Make sure you've got

mayonnaise ($1/2$ cup)

curry paste (2 teaspoons—check the small
    print on your curry paste, because some
    brands need cooking; if so, dry-fry the
    paste for a couple of minutes, or sizzle in
    the microwave)

❶ Mix the mayo and curry paste. Keeping 1 inch from the edge, spread a tortilla with a quarter of the curry-flavored mayonnaise.

❷ Add a quarter each of the turkey, cucumber, watercress, mango, and basil.

❸ If the wraps are to go, get ready a square of plastic wrap. Tuck in the sides of the wrap, then roll firmly to enclose the filling completely. Slice at an angle down the middle and wrap tightly with the plastic wrap. Continue to make the remaining wraps.

tuna in the Tunisian style

Serves 4 ● 10 to 20 minutes to prepare

Almost everything needed to make this dish can be found in the well-stocked, no-cook cupboard.

What you need

2 x 7-ounce cans tuna in oil, drained

2 x 7-ounce cans garbanzo beans, drained

2 miniature pickled lemons, thinly sliced and
  seeds discarded

bunch of fresh mint, chopped

1 lettuce, ideally romaine

Make sure you've got

16 to 24 pitted green or red olives, halved

8 strips of sun-dried tomato in oil, drained

1 garlic clove

ground coriander (1 teaspoon)

caraway seeds (1 teaspoon, optional)

harissa paste (1 teaspoon)

olive oil (2 tablespoons)

red-wine vinegar (2 tablespoons)

1 lemon, quartered

❶ Mix together the tuna, garbanzo beans, olives, pickled lemons, and mint.

❷ Make the dressing. In a blender or food processor, whiz together the sun-dried tomatoes, garlic, coriander, caraway, if using, harissa, olive oil, and vinegar—the dressing should be thick and sticky.

❸ Stir the dressing into the garbanzo beans.

❹ Arrange the lettuce leaves on 4 plates—in a starfish formation if you are feeling creative—and heap with the tuna and garbanzos. Serve with lemon quarters to squeeze over.

You can complete the salad up to a day ahead—the flavor even improves.

make it your own Serve this salad with couscous: Measure out $1^3/_4$ cups boiling water in a jug and add $1^1/_2$ teaspoons good-quality bouillon granules, 1 tablespoon olive oil, and $1^1/_3$ cups couscous. Leave for 10 minutes, stirring occasionally.

pan bagna *(simple)*

Serves 4 (easily halved or doubled) ● 15 to 20 minutes to prepare

This dish from Nice is a sort of salade niçoise sandwich. It is best made 2 to 24 hours in advance, and travels brilliantly wrapped in foil.

What you need

a loaf of country-style bread, preferably a thin
    round one about 8 inches in diameter

5 small, juicy tomatoes, sliced

large handful of basil (at least 20 leaves)

small handful of mint (at least 10 leaves)

5½ounces white tuna in water, or best-quality
    canned tuna, drained

1 shallot or 2 green onions, shredded

Make sure you've got

1 garlic clove, cut in half

extra-virgin olive oil (3 tablespoons)

red-wine vinegar (2 teaspoons)

capers (3 teaspoons), drained and rinsed

12 black olives, pitted and halved

8 anchovy fillets, preferably white
    anchovies in oil, drained and sliced

❶ Slice the loaf across its depth to make 2 thin round slices. Scrape out as much of the fluffy white bread in the middle as you can to make space for the filling.

❷ Rub the inside of each piece with garlic, to impart a subtle hint of the Riviera.

❸ Drizzle half the oil over one cut side of the bread, followed by half the vinegar. Scatter in half the tomatoes, season well, then top with half the herbs. Pile in the tuna, spreading it all over, then scatter with the shallot or green onions, capers, olives, and anchovies evenly. Add the remaining herbs and tomatoes. Drizzle the other piece of bread with the remaining oil and vinegar, and use as a lid for the sandwich.

❹ Squeeze together, wrap tightly in foil, and leave at room temperature for a couple of hours, or in the refrigerator overnight, but bring back to room temperature to eat.

You can make individual pan bagnas in rolls. Spread the filling right over the sandwich area so you don't end up with a barren patch around the perimeter.

make it your own
You can customize this in many different ways, although the use of good bread, the best tuna you can buy (look out for jars), salted capers (rather than pickled), good olives, and anchovies immediately makes it first class. ● Good additions or substitutions are chargrilled peppers, sun-dried tomatoes, fresh tarragon, and flavored oils.

lemony chicken couscous

Serves 4 (easily halved) ● 20 to 30 minutes to prepare

What you need

1 1/2 cups couscous

2 green onions, shredded

2 large tomatoes, cored, seeded, and roughly
    chopped

14 ounces cooked chargrilled chicken, cut into
    bite-size pieces

2 miniature preserved lemons, seeds and
    flesh discarded, finely sliced (1/4 of a large
    preserved lemon)

Make sure you've got

finely grated zest of 1/2 lemon

good-quality bouillon granules (1 1/2 teaspoons)

olive oil (1 tablespoons)

boiling water (1 3/4 cups)

harissa paste (1 to 2 teaspoons)

❶ Make the couscous by stirring the couscous, lemon zest, and bouillon granules together and pouring the olive oil and boiling water over. Cover loosely with plastic wrap and leave to stand for 10 minutes, fluffing up occasionally with a fork.

❷ Meanwhile, make the lemon chicken salad by stirring the green onions, tomatoes, and harissa until blended. Stir in the chicken and the preserved lemon slices.

❸ Arrange the couscous and the chicken on plates.

hoisin chicken, plums, and noodles

Serves 4 (easily doubled or halved) ● 15 to 25 minutes to prepare

Almost everything needed to make this dish can be found in the well-stocked, no-cook cupboard.

What you need
14ounces Chinese-flavored or
    maple-roast cooked chicken
9ounces fresh beansprouts
5 mi-cuit plums (see below), or soaked
    prunes

Make sure you've got
1 fresh red chili, seeded and thinly sliced
instant rice noodles (about 4ounces)
boiling water
rice-wine vinegar (2 teaspoons)
soy sauce (1 teaspoon)
hoisin sauce (2 tablespoons)
fresh ginger root (1/2 inch), grated
sunflower or other vegetable oil (4 tablespoons)

❶ Slice the chicken and put it in a bowl. Stir in the beansprouts and chili. Slice the plums or prunes and add to the chicken mixture.
❷ Snap the noodles in half or into thirds and put them into a bowl. Cover with boiling water and leave for 4 minutes, or as instructed on the package. Drain and mix into the chicken mixture.
❸ Meanwhile, mix the vinegar, soy sauce, hoisin sauce, ginger, and oil together. Stir into the chicken and noodles. Serve at once.

If you wash ginger root, there is no need to go through the fiddly process of peeling it—the skin is perfectly edible.

Mi-cuit plums are luscious plump semidried prunes. If you can't find them, you will need the moistest prunes you can find or, better still, ones that have been covered in boiling water and left to soak overnight.

tomato-mozzarella piémontaise

Serves 4 ● 10 to 20 minutes to prepare

This cross between a tomato and mozzarella salad and peppers piémontaise, in which peppers are stuffed with tomatoes and anchovies and baked, makes a great supper, but is also good as part of a buffet.

What you need

4 juicy tomatoes, halved through their equators
    and the seeds and pulp removed
2 ounces chargrilled peppers, sliced
4 ounces buffalo mozzarella, cubed
handful of fresh basil leaves

Make sure you've got

2 canned anchovies, rinsed, drained, and
    chopped
extra-virgin olive oil (1 tablespoon)
4 fat brown olives, pitted and halved

ahead

❶ Lay the tomato halves on a plate and season lightly.

❷ Mix the peppers, mozzarella, and anchovies together in a bowl. Pour the oil over, mix lightly, and spoon into the tomato halves—they should be full to overflowing. If convenient, you can leave the dish for up to 4 hours at this point.

at the last minute

❸ Casually scatter the basil leaves over the tomatoes. Top each with half an olive and serve. If the sun isn't shining, imagine it is.

make it your own Spanish piquillo peppers are great for this dish. ● If you have a lemon- or basil-scented extra-virgin olive oil, this is the time to use it.

Thai beef and cucumber

Serves 4 (easily doubled) ● 10 to 20 minutes to prepare

This is an example of fusion food, where New York (pastrami) meets Bangkok (everything else). If you want to make this dish look effortless, you can measure everything, cut the pastrami, and slice the vegetables an hour or two ahead—but don't assemble until just before serving.

What you need
4 ounces pastrami (from the deli)
1 cucumber (about 1 pound) peeled, halved,
    seeds scooped out with a spoon, and thinly
    sliced
1 shallot, very thinly sliced
5 ounces crisp lettuce leaves
handful of fresh cilantro and of mint, roughly
    chopped

Make sure you've got
1 small fresh red chili, very thinly sliced
honey (1 tablespoon)
Japanese rice wine or dry sherry
    (3 tablespoons)
good pinch chili flakes

ahead
❶ Slice the pastrami at an angle into strips. Mix with the cucumber, shallot, and sliced chili, using your fingers to separate the thin slices of pastrami.

at the last minute
❷ Whisk the honey, rice wine or sherry, and chili flakes together, and fold into the meat mixture.
❸ Arrange the lettuce on a platter. Spoon the meat mixture over the middle, drizzling any dressing left in the bowl over the lettuce. Serve covered with a blanket of cilantro and mint.

toasting success

When it comes to bread-based snacks, the Italians know every trick in the book. Bruschetta is a Tuscan invention—originally used to test the quality of the new-season's olive oil. Thick slices of Italian bread—authentically country bread such as pugliese—are toasted on both sides in a toaster or under a broiler, then rubbed with a cut garlic clove, drizzled with extra-virgin olive oil, and sprinkled with coarse salt. The toast should be crisp on the outside and soft in the middle, and ideally enjoyed hot from the broiler. Toppings are not strictly necessary, but, if you are offering them, choose bread with a strong crust, or plan to eat them with a knife and fork. Toppings should have strong flavors and contrasting colors—let everyone help themselves.

1 use your best oil This is an occasion when specialty oils—extra-virgin, or oil infused with lemon or basil—will come into their own (after all, bruschetta was "invented" to showcase their flavors). Don't mask the taste of these extra-fine oils with toppings, but don't forget to rub the bread with garlic and sprinkle on some coarse salt.

2 Catalan bruschettas Although this bruschetta variation is practiced all over Italy, I first came across it in Spain. The idea is to give the bruschetta a final rub with the cut side of a super-ripe, juicy tomato. Season and serve as is, or as a base for other toppings.

3 tapenade bruschettas Spread the bruschettas with tapenade or olive paste and top with wedges of plum tomato or thick slices of cucumber, cut at an angle.

4 smoked cheddar, tomato, and basil bruschettas Put a thin slice of smoked cheddar on a bruschetta, top with a slice of tomato or strip of sun-dried tomato, and a basil leaf.

5 pesto and mozzarella bruschetta Spread bruschetta with pesto sauce—classic basil, olive, or red pepper—and top with a slice of fresh mozzarella cheese.

6 prosciutto and fig bruschettas Spread bruschettas with Italian Dolcelatte cheese and top with a curl of prosciutto (or another thinly sliced smoked meat, such as turkey) and a quarter of a fresh fig. A leaf of purple basil is a pretty finishing touch.

7 pâté and pepper bruschettas Spread bruschettas with a coarse pâté and top with a slice of chargrilled pepper from a jar of antipasto—or a slice of piquillo pepper.

8 crostini Crostini are usually made from finely textured ciabatta bread, or slices of French baguette. More petite than bruschetta, they can be untoasted or toasted, and are usually served cold as an appetizer or canapé, spread with something tasty, rather than acting as a base for things piled on top. Sometimes they are toasted until completely crisp and then rubbed with garlic and drizzled with oil like bruschetta—and this is how I like them.

9 creamy Gorgonzola crostini Mix Gorgonzola with an equal quantity of mascarpone. Spread on the crostini and top with a teaspoon of tapenade or chopped olives, and snipped chives.

10 pizza-flavored crostini Lay a chopped anchovy on a crostini and mash it. Top with slices of juicy tomato and a sliver of Parmesan.

prosciutto and fig bruschetta

pizza-flavored crostini

creamy Gorgonzola crostini

pâté and pepper bruschetta

glamorous
nibbles
and appetizers

no need to spend ages making elaborate
canapés and first courses. Just assemble
clever combinations of food and
present them beautifully—the
spirit of no-cooking

smoked haddock carpaccio
Serves 4 ● 10 minutes to prepare (but start a good hour ahead)

Here smoked haddock is very thinly sliced to look delicate and elegant, resembling smoked salmon.

What you need

7 ounce piece of undyed smoked haddock
    fillet, preferably the thick part of the fillet

for the dressing

2 green onions, shredded
small handful of fresh parsley, finely chopped

Make sure you've got

capers (1 tablespoon), chopped
extra-virgin olive oil (1 tablespoon)
$\frac{1}{2}$ lemon
pepper

ahead
❶ Put the haddock in the freezer for 15 to 20 minutes to make it easier to slice.
❷ Sharpen your knife. Trim the edges off the fillet so you are left with only the fleshy middle section; discard the edges. (You might have as much as 2 ounces of waste, but don't worry, it's worth it.)
❸ Slice down into the fillet, against the grain, to make long, very thin rectangles of fish fillet. You should get 30 to 40 very thin slices from the fillet. Lay these on a large plate to cover it completely. Try to scrape the slices from the skin as you go, or trim the skin off each slice and discard the skin.

at the last minute
❹ About 20 minutes before serving, scatter with the green onions, parsley, capers, olive oil, and lemon juice, one by one, finishing with plenty of black pepper.
❺ Serve accompanied by bread and butter.

This dish can only be made with undyed smoked haddock, which is a pale creamy color. The bright yellow dyed type should be avoided.

make it your own British food writer Henrietta Green, who taught me this recipe, tells me you can treat cold roast beef (preferably rare), chicken, and turkey in exactly the same way.

potted shrimp marinara

Serves 6 (easily halved or multiplied) ● 10 to 20 minutes to prepare (needs 2 hours to chill)

This is an updated variation on an old-fashioned British classic.

What you need

9 ounces medium or large shelled shrimp,
    thawed and drained if frozen

1 tablespoon red pepper or other red pesto

Make sure you've got

butter (1 stick, ¼ lb)

1 anchovy fillet, rinsed (optional)

tomato paste or sun-dried tomato paste (1 tablespoon)

Worcestershire sauce

Tabasco sauce

salt and pepper

bread for toast, to serve

ahead

❶ Melt the butter.

❷ Roughly chop the shrimp. Finely chop the anchovy and mix it with the tomato paste, pesto, a splash each of Worcestershire and Tabasco sauce, and some seasoning. Stir in the butter.

❸ You can serve these in ramekin dishes or unmold them onto individual plates. If you are planning to unmold the potted shrimp, line the bottoms of 6 small (½ cup) ramekins with little circles of parchment paper. (If planning to serve the shrimp in the ramekins, there is no need to do this.) Pack in the shrimp mixture and chill for a couple of hours until set, or up to 24 hours.

at the last minute

❹ Either serve the shrimp in the ramekins, or run a knife around the edge and invert them onto plates. If they don't come out easily, dip the bottoms briefly in boiling water and try again. Peel off the lining paper.

Serve with lots of freshly made toast on which to spread the shrimp.

shrimp and melon cocktails

Serves 4 ● 15 to 30 minutes to prepare, depending on your melon-balling skills

If you plan to serve this for large numbers it is a bit arduous making the melon balls. Buy them, if you can, already prepared at a salad bar or deli counter.

What you need
7 ounces shelled shrimp, thawed, if
    necessary, drained and dried
1½ pounds green or orange melon flesh, cut
    into small cubes or balls (or 9 ounces
    prepared melon balls)
crisp lettuce leaves

Make sure you've got
dried chili flakes (¼ teaspoon)
mayonnaise (½ cup)
salt and pepper
smoked paprika for dusting

ahead
❶ Mix the shrimp and melon together, then leave to drain in a small strainer set over a bowl. You can do this a day ahead, but leave the shrimp and melon in the refrigerator.

at the last minute
❷ Discard the shrimp liquid that has collected in the bowl. Mix the chili flakes into the mayonnaise, then fold into the shrimp and melon.
❸ Arrange the lettuce on plates and season lightly. Arrange the shrimp and melon cocktail on top, dust with smoked paprika, and serve.

make it your own If you use 2 small melons, you can serve the cocktail in the hollowed-out shells, rather than on lettuce leaves. Leave the melon halves to drain upside down.
● For the slightly more adventurous, whisk 1 teaspoon curry paste into the mayonnaise. (See the note about curry paste on page 14.)

smoked salmon savvy

One of the most wonderful of no-cook treats, smoked salmon is glamorous, tasty, and versatile. It is thin and delicate enough to be used as a wrapping for other foods, and makes an attractive focal point in its own right. Smoked salmon varies hugely in quality: The best is translucent, firm, and with widely spaced markings. Unless you wish to impress with your knife skills, always buy it sliced. Trimmings are cheaper, and useful in many dishes.

1 lunch to go Spread a tortilla with 1 tablespoon mayonnaise and top with some smoked salmon, lots of cress, and sliced tomato. Squeeze some lemon juice over, grind some pepper over, tuck in the sides, and roll up. Cut in half and eat.

2 fabulous finger food Whip a ⅔ cup heavy (whipping) cream, crème fraîche, or sour cream until just beginning to thicken. Add 1 tablespoon grated horseradish or horseradish sauce and 1 tablespoon lemon juice. Roughly chop 4 ounces shelled cooked jumbo shrimp and fold in, season. Lay out the salmon slices one by one (you will need 9 ounces), top with a dollop of the cream mixture at the narrow   end and roll up to make short, thick rolls. Dust the ends with paprika before serving—enough for 6 as a canapé or appetizers.

3 glitzy canapé Cut 7 ounces smoked salmon into 3½-inch squares. Put a teaspoon of Boursin (either the pepper or garlic-and-fine-herb type) in the middle of each. Gather at the top and tie with a chive. For 8 bite-size purses, you will need 3½ ounces Boursin cheese, plus 8 stout chives.

4 glamorous garnish Use 1 pound salmon fillet. Cut 2 ounces of smoked salmon into thin strips and arrange as a lattice on the cooked salmon fillet, tucking the ends underneath. Serve with a simple sauce of chopped fresh dill stirred into crème fraîche or sour cream.

5 goat cheese bites Use a 3½-ounce log of goat cheese and wrap it in plastic wrap. Roll it out until 1¼ inch in diameter and about 7 inches long. Wrap the cheese in smoked salmon (you'll need about 3 ounces) and chill for at least an hour or overnight. Sharpen your knife and slice it into 10 to 12 bites.

6 stylish pappadams Pile 1 teaspoon bought tzatziki (or make your own from a 2-inch piece cucumber, trimmed and sliced, some chopped mint, a scrap of garlic and $2/3$ cup thick plain yogurt) into the middle of mini-pappadams. Top a third with a twist of smoked salmon, a third with a shelled cooked jumbo shrimp, and a third with a spoonful of Avruga (herring) caviar. (For 20 mini-pappadams, you will need 4 tablespoons tzatziki, 2 ounces smoked salmon, 1$1/2$ ounces shrimp, 7 to 8 teaspoons of Avruga.). Do this at the last minute or they become soft.

7 toasted treat Spread toasted crumpets, or English muffins, with mascarpone, then top with smoked salmon—and Avruga (herring or lumpfish) caviar, if you have some. For 4 crumpets you will need about 3 ounces mascarpone and the same of smoked salmon. Great for brunch.

8 crunchy with cocktails Finely chop 2 ounces smoked salmon (or smoked salmon pieces) with a little cilantro and ground black pepper. Divide 2 or 3 heads of Belgian endives into leaves and put a teaspoon into each leaf.

9 posh appetizers Line 6 small ramekins or coffee cups with plastic wrap, then line with smoked salmon, slicing into strips as necessary and leaving enough hanging over to fold over the top (you will need 7 to 10$1/2$ ounces). Put 10 ounces smoked trout fillets in a processor with 1 tablespoon of chopped fresh dill, $2/3$ cup cottage cheese, $2/3$ cup sour cream, and the juice of $1/2$ lemon. Season well with pepper (it probably won't need any salt), then spoon into the ramekins and fold over the smoked salmon. Chill overnight, then turn out, peel off the plastic wrap and serve as a first course. This makes enough for 6.

10 salad in a flash Toss strips of smoked salmon and jumbo shrimp into a lettuce, cucumber, and tomato salad. Grate a little lemon zest over, dress with a lemon-flavored vinaigrette, and scatter with basil leaves or snipped chives.

toasted treats

crunchy with cocktails

salad in a flash

posh appetizer

fruity anchoïade

Serves 4 as a spread or dip ● 5 to 10 minutes to prepare

What you need
4 plump dried figs
1 fresh red bell pepper, roughly chopped
good handful of fresh parsley

Make sure you've got
extra-virgin olive oil (2 tablespoons)
6 anchovies, rinsed and squeezed dry
squeeze of lemon juice

❶ Mix everything together and whiz in a food processor.
❷ Serve with bread or crudités. Ask guests to guess what's in the dip.

Salted anchovies, which you can buy in cans and jars, have a more pungent taste than those in oil, and I prefer them for this recipe.

make it your own **In true Middle Eastern style, you can add all sorts of exotica to the basic recipe—rosewater, a scrap of preserved lemon, a flick of orange zest—to heighten the mystery.**

green anchoïade

Serves 4 as a spread or dip ● 5 to 10 minutes to prepare

What you need
handful of mixed fresh herbs, including
    parsley, mint, and basil
1 tablespoon pine nuts

Make sure you've got
1 large garlic clove
2 anchovies, drained
1 lemon
extra-virgin olive oil (¾ cup)
salt and pepper
capers (1 tablespoon), drained, rinsed, and chopped
    (optional)

❶ In a food processor, whiz the garlic until finely chopped, then add the herbs and anchovies.
❷ With the motor still running, add the juice from the lemon and the oil with some seasoning (Add salt with care because the anchovies are salty) to form a beautiful green emulsion.
❸ Stir in the capers, if you like them, and the pine nuts.

rum tapenade

Serves 4 or more as part of a dip selection ● 10 to 15 minutes to prepare

What you need

2 green onions

1 tablespoon dark rum

pita breads, to serve

Make sure you've got

anchovy fillets (1 ounce), rinsed

1 garlic clove

good pinch dried chili flakes

black olives (4 ounces), pitted

extra-virgin olive oil (2 tablespoons)

squeeze of lemon juice

❶ In a food processor, whiz the green onions, anchovies, garlic, and chili flakes until mashed.

❷ Add the olives and whiz again until these are coarsely chopped.

❸ With the motor still running, add the oil, lemon juice, and rum.

❹ Serve with toasted pita breads.

cannellini bean hummus

Serves 6 or more as part of a dip selection ● 10 to 15 minutes to prepare

What you need

1 green onion

2 x 7-ounce cans cannellini beans, drained and
    rinsed

2 tablespoons tahini sauce (or even peanut butter)

pita breads, to serve

Make sure you've got

1 garlic clove

olive oil (2 tablespoons, plus more for drizzling)

1 slice (1 ounce) white bread, soaked in water
    and immediately squeezed out

grated zest of $1/2$ lemon

ground coriander ($1/2$ teaspoon)

ground cumin (1 teaspoon, plus more for dusting)

❶ In a food processor, whiz the green onion and garlic until finely chopped.

❷ Add the beans and process until a dry puree forms, then add the tahini, oil, bread, lemon zest, and spices.

❸ With the motor still running, add 3 to 4 tablespoons cold water to lighten the texture.

❹ Spread thinly over a medium-size plate. Drizzle some oil over and dust with cumin. Serve with toasted pita breads.

fruity anchoïade

rum tapenade

cannellini bean hummus

green anchoïade

smoked duck with papaya

Serves 4 as a dainty fusion-style appetizer ● 10 to 20 minutes to prepare

What you need

1 ripe papaya

1 smoked duck breast, about 8 ounces

Make sure you've got

soy sauce

Tabasco sauce

Worcestershire sauce

for the sauce

$2/3$ cup coconut cream

1 teaspoon creamed coconut (from a block,
    optional)

finely grated zest of $1/4$ lime

$1/2$ teaspoon tamarind paste (from a jar, optional)

12 fresh basil leaves

ahead

❶ Peel the papaya with a small knife and cut it in half. Discard the caviarlike seeds and slice the flesh neatly. Put on a plate, cover with plastic wrap and chill until ready to eat.

❷ Slice the fat off the duck breast and discard. Cut the flesh into thin, neat slices. Cover with plastic wrap and chill.

❸ Whisk the coconut cream and creamed coconut together until creamy. Add the lime zest, tamarind, a splash each of soy sauce, the Tabasco and Worcestershire sauces, and the basil leaves, torn if large. Chill until ready to serve.

at the last minute

❹ Pour the sauce over 4 small plates (this is called "flooding" the plates). Arrange the duck and papaya on the sauce and serve.

Papaya is a good-natured fruit, in that it will remain ripe without "going off" for up to four days.

classic celery-root rémoulade with prosciutto

Serves 4 (easily doubled, but cutting the celery root is a bit of bore for larger numbers) ● 20 to 30 minutes to prepare

What you need

1 pound fresh celery root

3½ ounces prosciutto di Parma

Make sure you've got

½ lemon

boiling water to cover

mayonnaise (½ cup, bought or homemade, see
     page 87)

mustard (2 teaspoons, preferably wholegrain)

capers (1 teaspoon), rinsed

2 gherkins, rinsed and chopped

good bunch of fresh parsley or tarragon, chopped

pepper

ahead

❶ Squeeze the lemon half into a large heatproof bowl. Peel the celery root, removing all the brown bits. Slice it thinly, then slice these again into matchsticks, putting them into the bowl and tossing in the lemon as you go. (Take a tip from professional food stylists and discard any mis-shapes or stubs—although thriftiness is to be applauded, they will make the finished dish look scruffy.)

❷ Cover with boiling water, put a lid or plate over the bowl, and leave for 5 minutes. Drain the celery root and refresh in cold water, then drain again and dry on paper towels.

❸ Make the dressing by mixing together the mayonnaise, mustard, capers, gherkins, and parsley or tarragon. Toss the celery root in the dressing, making sure all is covered. You can leave it for up to 4 hours at this point.

at the last minute

❹ Cut the prosciutto into bite-size strips and arrange these, ribbon style, around the edge of the plate. Heap the salad in the middle. Grind some pepper over and serve.

watermelon, feta, and nut salad (simple)

Serves 4 as a side dish or first course (easily halved or multiplied for large gatherings) ● 10 to 15 minutes to prepare (presentation is important)

Middle Eastern in origin, this is one of the prettiest salads I know. It looks best in a large glass bowl or individual glass dishes.

What you need
18 ounces fresh watermelon
   (15 ounces prepared weight)
5 ounces feta cheese
1/4 cup chopped toasted hazelnuts

Make sure you've got
olive oil (2 tablespoons)
squeeze of lemon juice
pepper

❶ Dice the watermelon flesh into neat $3/4$-inch cubes. Cut the feta into slightly smaller cubes.
❷ Toss these together in a bowl. Add the nuts, oil, and plenty of black pepper.
❸ If you make this more than a few minutes ahead, the watermelon gives off a lot of water, so at the last minute transfer the salad to your serving bowl with a draining spoon. Squeeze some lemon juice over and serve.

The quality of the feta is important: Some of the packed types can be dry and salty. It is far better to buy it loose in oil from the cheese counter.

make it your own
If you do buy feta in oil, use the oil in the dressing. Alternatively use lemon-infused olive oil. ● Use sliced pistachios or pumpkin seeds instead of the hazelnuts.

LEFT classic celery-root rémoulade with Prosciutto **ABOVE** watermelon, feta, and nut salad

fresh cream of avocado soup

Serves 6 (easily halved) ● 15 to 25 minutes to prepare, plus chilling and an extra 5 minutes if making the salsa

A ravishing pale green in color, this is the prettiest soup I know. You can see why decorators went for bathroom suites this shade in the 1970s. It may seem anathema to add water to something that is already very subtle in flavor, but the water emulsifies with the avocado to give a divine texture. The soup is very rich, so serve it in small portions.

What you need
2 green onions
4 fresh avocados, pitted and peeled
6 fresh mint leaves
1$^{1}/_{4}$cups light cream
snipped chives or salsa (see below)

Make sure you've got
2 garlic cloves
$^{1}/_{2}$ lemon
Tabasco sauce
Worcestershire sauce
salt and pepper

❶ Blitz the green onions and garlic in a food processor until smashed.

❷ Add the avocado flesh, mint, a squeeze of lemon juice, a splash each of Tabasco and Worcestershire sauce, and plenty of seasoning.

❸ Pour in the cream and whiz, then pulse in 1$^{1}/_{2}$cups water, which will give the texture an almost ethereal lightness: The soup should be as thick as semiwhipped cream; add a little extra water, if necessary.

❹ Chill the soup for an hour. If leaving longer, squeeze a little extra lemon juice over the surface to preserve the fresh jade green.

❺ Serve very cold, with snipped chives or a blob of salsa.

Make a quick salsa by roughly processing a green onion with $^{1}/_{2}$ red chili, $^{1}/_{2}$ red bell pepper and a medium-size tomato, making sure you keep some texture. Season well and divide between the six bowls. This makes about $^{3}/_{4}$ cup.

make it your own You can give this more of a Mexican theme by serving it with corn tortilla chips.

cucumber and watercress vichyssoise

Serves 4 ● 10 to 15 minutes to prepare, but chilling

Seasoned well and served very cold, this makes a rich and creamy start to a meal.

What you need
5 green onions, including about 2 inches of
    green top, roughly cut up
3 or 4 sprigs of fresh mint
3 ounces fresh watercress
1 cucumber (about 1 pound), peeled (takes a
    second with a potato peeler), halved with
    the seeds scooped out, and cut into chunks
²/₃ cup light cream
fresh snipped chives, to garnish

Make sure you've got
¹/₂ garlic clove
salt and pepper
¹/₂ lemon
dry sherry (2 tablespoons)
nutmeg

❶ In your food processor, blitz the garlic as finely as possible, then add the green onions and mint. Wipe down the sides with a spatula, then add the watercress, followed by the cucumber. Process until it forms a wet paste.

❷ Add the cream. Season well with salt, pepper, the juice from the lemon half, the sherry, and freshly grated nutmeg to taste.

❸ Chill for at least an hour, or up to 24 hours. Serve in small bowls with snipped chives.

Chilled or frozen mixtures require much more seasoning or sweetening than those served at room temperature or hot. (If you have tasted melted ice cream, you will know how sweet it seems.) In this case, check the soup is well seasoned before it goes into the refrigerator and again before serving.

sun-blushed gazpacho

Serves 4 (easily multiplied—you can serve mini-portions in coffee cups or shot glasses as an appetizer)

● **10 to 20 minutes to prepare**

This makes an amazingly beautiful, sunset-colored soup.

What you need

1 ounce sun-blushed or sun-dried tomatoes

12 ounces good ripe tomatoes

2 green onions

about a 4-inch piece of cucumber

To garnish

chopped green bell pepper

chopped seeded cucumber

strips of sun-blushed tomato

strips of chargrilled red pepper

pitted green and black olives

Make sure you've got

crustless good white bread (4 ounces)

1 garlic clove

½ small red chili

sherry or red-wine vinegar (2 tablespoons)

extra-virgin olive oil (2 tablespoons)

salt and pepper

❶ Put the bread in a bowl of water and then squeeze it out gently. Put it in a food processor.

❷ Chop the sun-blushed or sun-dried tomatoes into the processor, then add the fresh tomatoes, green onions and garlic. Peel the cucumber, halve along the middle, and scrape out the seeds. Roughly chop and add to processor along with chili, vinegar, and oil. Whiz for a couple of minutes until really smooth, scraping down the sides a couple of times. Taste and adjust the seasoning, then chill for at least 30 minutes. You can make this a day ahead if convenient.

❸ To serve, check the seasoning again, because being as cold as this tends to dull flavors. You can thin the soup, if you wish, with ice water, but I like it thick. Some cooks strain it, but I again I prefer it *au naturel*. Serve with the garnishes.

make it your own The garnishes are an important feature of gazpacho, and you can lay them all out on a platter for guests to help themselves. The only proviso is that they should be cut small enough to be eaten with a soupspoon.

cheese and nut balls (simple)

Makes 20 cocktail-size balls ● 15 to 20 minutes to prepare (make the mixture ahead)

These ingenious little mouthfuls make perfect snacks to serve with drinks.

What you need

$\frac{1}{2}$cup ricotta cheese

$\frac{2}{3}$cup grated Double Gloucester or cheddar
    cheese

1$\frac{1}{2}$tablespoons chopped toasted hazelnuts

Make sure you've got

Tabasco sauce

Worcestershire sauce

ahead

❶ In a bowl, mix the cheeses with a splash each of Tabasco and Worcestershire sauce, then chill in the refrigerator. If you are in a hurry, spread the mixture out thinly—it will chill faster.

at the last minute

❷ Put the nuts in a bowl. Take a teaspoon of the mixture and roll into a small ball. It is tempting to make them big, especially if you are impatient by nature, but they are much nicer small, no larger than marbles.

❸ Drop the balls into the nuts, roll them around until they are coated, and put them on a serving plate. Continue shaping cheese balls until all the mixture is used.

make it your own
You can use another hard cheese instead of the Double Gloucester or cheddar; smoked cheddar packs a punch. ● You can use walnuts instead or hazelnuts, but they need to be very finely chopped. ● If you want to make tricolor balls, you can coat one-third of the balls with nuts, one-third with finely chopped herbs, and one-third with paprika. You will, however, find the nutty ones get scoffed first.

chilled Parmesan and chive soufflé

Serves 6 ● 10 to 20 minutes to prepare (plus a 10-minute wait for the gelatin to set; make this at least 2—and up to 24—hours ahead)

This is an elegant and understated dish. Don't turn the page when you see the word gelatin—it really isn't difficult to use, and it's worth the trouble.

What you need
2 teaspoons unflavored powdered gelatin
    (about 2/3 of an envelop)
2 ounces Parmesan cheese
handful of fresh chives
1 1/4 cups heavy (whipping) cream

Make sure you've got
good-quality bouillon granules (1 teaspoon)
boiling water (2/3 cup)
2 eggs
pinch of salt
cayenne pepper
paprika for dusting
bread for toast, to serve

ahead

❶ Mix the gelatin and bouillon granules in a bowl. Pour the boiling water over and whisk well until the gelatin dissolves and is smooth; leave to cool to room temperature.

❷ Meanwhile, grate the cheese and snip the chives. Separate the eggs and beat the egg whites in a large bowl with a pinch of salt until they form soft peaks, which fall when you remove the beaters. (Use the yolks for mayonnaise, page 87.)

❸ In another bowl, whip the cream until just stiff, but not firm. Fold the cream into the egg whites, together with the cheese, chives, and a pinch of cayenne.

❹ Pour into a 1-quart soufflé dish and leave to set.

at the last minute

❺ Dust with paprika and serve with hot toast.

make it your own Vary the herbs—finely chopped chervil or tarragon go well.

memorable
main courses

nowadays you can readily buy excellent already-cooked
chicken, turkey, duck, and even seafood.
Think exciting main-course salads, captivating cold
collations, and even the no-cook's answer
to take-out

lobster and avocado surprise
Serves 8 ● 30 to 40 minutes to prepare

This sounds extraordinary, but is actually quite sensational and delicious, as well as psychedelic looking.

What you need

2 ounces fresh strawberries

4 small (1 pound) boiled lobsters (to give
  about 10½ ounces lobster meat)

2 ripe avocados

2 tablespoons slivered almonds, toasted

Make sure you've got

1 lemon

sunflower oil (⅔ cup)

salt and pepper

ahead
❶ Make the dressing by hulling the strawberries and putting them in a food processor with the juice of half the lemon (save the rest for later), the oil, and plenty of salt and pepper.
❷ Pick the lobster meat from the lobster shells and claws (unless you have an official lobster pick, a skewer helps). Cover and refrigerate.

at the last minute
❸ Halve the avocados and pull out the pits. Slice the flesh with the skin still on (and not cutting through the skin), then use a spatula to lever out the flesh—it should come away in neat slices.
❹ Arrange the pieces of lobster on a large serving plate, brighter side facing up, and nestle the avocado slices among them. Drizzle with the strawberry sauce and scatter with the almonds.

make it your own You can serve this salad in the lobster shells—one each. Lay alternating slices of avocado and lobster in the shells and drizzle with the sauce.

shrimp, mango, and spinach salad

Serves 4 (easily halved or doubled) ● 10 to 15 minutes to prepare (the mango and dressing can be prepared ahead, but assemble the salad at the table)

This glamorous main course salad has a distinctly Oriental feel.

What you need
3/4-inch cube of fresh root ginger, grated or
    finely chopped
4 ounces young spinach leaves
7 ounces shelled shrimp, thawed if frozen
1 large mango, peeled, pitted, and thinly sliced
1 shallot or 2 green onions, sliced very thinly

Make sure you've got
dry sherry (1 tablespoon)
1 orange (finely grated zest and juice of 1/2 of it)
sunflower oil (3 tablespoons)
dark sesame oil (1 teaspoon)
salt and pepper

ahead
❶ Make the dressing by whisking the gingerroot, sherry, orange zest and juice, and the oils in a bowl. Season lightly.

at the last minute
❷ When everyone is at the table, lay the spinach in a bowl and top with the shrimp, mango, and shallot or green onions. Pour the dressing over and fold together gently.

You can buy sliced mango, which saves a lot of slippery effort. You will need about 7 ounces for this recipe.

make it your own Shelled tiger prawns or jumbo shrimp make this dish more luxurious.
● Use papaya instead of mango.

salmon with watercress mousseline

Serves 6 (easily halved, or doubled for a large party) ● 10 to 20 minutes to prepare

For this dish, you can buy poached salmon steaks, or even whole sides of salmon. Allow 4 ounces per person.

What you need
1¹/₂ ounces watercress, plus a bouquet of
　beautiful sprigs, to garnish
¹/₂ cup fromage blanc
6 poached salmon steaks or fillets (see
　introduction)

Make sure you've got
2 egg yolks
light olive oil or sunflower oil (7 tablespoons)

ahead
❶ Put the watercress in a blender or food processor and blitz to a smoothish puree. Add the egg yolks and, scraping down the side as necessary, whiz to a green paste. With the motor running, start adding the oil, initially drop by drop, then in a thin stream. When all the oil is incorporated, stir or pulse in the fromage blanc and season well. Transfer to a bowl.

at the last minute
❷ Put the salmon steaks on plates and generously spoon the sauce over. Add a top-knot of watercress to each plate and serve.

make it your own Don't tell a soul, but adding 2 teaspoons of Pernod or Ricard to the sauce gives it a haunting herby flavor. No one will guess, but they will wonder what you've done. ● Instead of the watercress sprigs for a garnish, you can halve a small tomato, discard the seeds and pulp, and cut the flesh into tiny dice. Dot this over the sauce and serve.

smoked salmon and cucumber torte

Serves 6 to 8 (excellent doubled for a grand affair) ● **30 to 40 minutes to prepare (but not much actual work)**

This combination is rich and stylish. Serve it in wedges with brown bread and butter and lemon quarters.

What you need
9 ounces cucumber (1 small cucumber, or
    $\frac{1}{2}$ a big one)
scant 1 cup crème fraîche
plenty of chopped dill
7 ounces sliced smoked salmon

Make sure you've got
1 lemon (finely grated zest and juice of)
horseradish sauce (2 teaspoons)
pepper

ahead
❶ To stop the cucumber becoming watery, peel it with a potato peeler, then cut it down the middle and scrape out the seeds of each half with a spoon. Slice each half in half again to make 4 long pieces, then slice these to about $\frac{1}{8}$ inch thick and lay them on a piece of paper towel. Sprinkle with salt and leave for 15 minutes to an hour, covered with more paper towels.

❷ Meanwhile, stand the ring of your smallest loose-bottomed cake pan (you won't need the base) on a plate to act as a mold.

❸ In a largish bowl, beat the crème fraîche, lemon zest, horseradish sauce, and dill with plenty of black pepper. Crème fraîche varies, so add 1 to 2 tablespoons lemon juice to relax the cream, if necessary, as you don't want it too stiff.

❹ Cut the salmon slices into ribbons about $\frac{3}{4}$ inch thick. (It might be easiest to slice right through the salmon and any interleaving pieces of plastic film, but make sure you get rid of all the plastic.) Then cut the ribbons at an angle into bite-size pieces.

❺ Rinse the cucumber to get rid of the salt and pat dry. Fold the cucumber slices into the cream with the salmon pieces until well mixed, then spoon into the mold.

❻ Cover and refrigerate for at least 30 minutes, or overnight if you wish.

at the last minute
❼ Blot the plate with paper towels, if necessary. Run a blunt-edged knife around the edge of the cake pan and remove.

shop & serve suppers

When you don't feel like cooking, there is no need to—just put together a clever combo of ingredients and enjoy an effortless, tasty light meal. The following ideas are all generally intended for one, but are not too specific on quantities as you can vary these according to appetite, and easily scale them up to serve a couple or more.

1 insalata tricolore Scatter basil leaves over a platter and add buffalo mozzarella balls, fresh cherry tomatoes, and black olives. Drizzle with extra-virgin or basil-scented olive oil.

2 avocado and feta salad Pit, peel, and cut an avocado into large chunks. Arrange the avocado chunks on a serving plate with 3 ounces cubed feta and some black olives. Squeeze lemon juice over and eat with pita bread.

3 Italian plowman's Arrange 4 juicy plum tomatoes, a whole mozzarella, and half a dozen balsamic-marinated baby onions on a plate. Drizzle with lemon-infused olive oil and mop up with ciabatta bread.

4 ham with grapes and cheese toasts Roll up slices of Serrano or other top-quality cured or cooked ham. Serve with seedless black grapes and slices of toast spread with cream cheese.

5 fig rollups Cover bought crepes with prosciutto or other good ham, scatter with Dolcelatte cheese and fresh fig, both cut into small pieces, and arugula leaves. Drizzle with extra-virgin olive oil. Roll tightly and slice in half.

LEFT shrimp and mayonnaise leaves

BELOW Mediterranean vegetable platter

ABOVE goat cheese with endive and cherries

RIGHT gravlax with cucumber

6 shrimp and mayonnaise leaves Lay out some romaine lettuce leaves and add shelled cooked jumbo shrimp and a mini-dollop of mayo to each. Squeeze lemon juice over and snip chives over. Eat.

7 goat cheese with endive and cherries Surround a whole fresh goat cheese with crunchy endive leaves. Sprinkle fresh cherries around the plate. Eat using a knife and your fingers.

8 Mediterranean vegetable platter Drain 2 ounces each of preserved chargrilled peppers, artichokes, and sun-dried tomatoes and put on a plate. Snip some basil leaves over, squeeze some lemon juice over and enjoy with focaccia bread.

9 gravlax with cucumber Arrange thin slices of gravlax (about 4 ounces) and cucumber on a plate and drizzle sour cream and chopped dill over. Scoop up with buttered rye or German-style bread.

10 pear and Stilton salad Slice a fresh pear and 2 ounces Stilton cheese over lightly dressed watercress. Scatter with walnut halves and eat with a knife and fork.

turkey tonnato

Serves 4 to 6 ● 15 to 20 minutes to prepare

This is a variation on the classic Roman *vitello tonnato*, in which thin slices of veal are covered with smooth tuna mayonnaise. Poultry with fish may seem like an odd combination, but this is a sumptuous dish.

What you need

14 ounces cooked turkey from the delicatessen
    counter, thickly sliced, or 4 cooked
    skinless, boneless chicken breast halves

To decorate

pitted olives

extra anchovies, rinsed and sliced

freshly chopped parsley

Make sure you've got

2 egg yolks

juice of $\frac{1}{2}$ lemon

Dijon mustard (2 teaspoons)

sunflower oil (1$\frac{1}{4}$ cups)

tuna in oil (7 ounces), drained

3 canned anchovy fillets, rinsed

capers (2 tablespoons, plus extra to
    garnish), rinsed

ahead

❶ Make a mayonnaise by putting the egg yolks, lemon juice, and mustard in the small bowl of your food processor. With the motor running, start adding the oil literally drop by drop; once the mix starts to look thick and gloopy, add the oil in a thin stream.

❷ When all the oil is incorporated, add the tuna, anchovies, and capers, and whiz until smooth. Taste and season—it might need a little more lemon juice, plus pepper and possibly salt. It might also need a little water to get a good spreading consistency.

❸ Cut the turkey into slices about the size of a dollar bill; if using chicken, slice each chicken breast horizontally into 3 pieces.

❹ Spread a thin layer of the mayonnaise over a large, flat serving plate. Selecting the less well-shaped slices, arrange half the turkey in one layer on the mayonnaise.

❺ Spread with half the remaining mayo, then arrange the remaining turkey slices on top, like the blades of a propeller. Finish by covering everything with the remaining mayo.

at the last minute

❻ Decorate with the capers, olives, and anchovies, then dust with parsley.

fruity almond chicken (simple)

Serves 4 (easily multiplied) ● **10 to 20 minutes to prepare, plus chilling**

Pretty, stylish, and very tasty, this is a great dish for a summer lunch party.

What you need
4 cooked skinless and boneless
    chicken breast halves (about 14 ounces)
4 green onions, shredded
2ounces bought crispy fried bacon
1/3cup roasted unsalted almonds, halved
snipped fresh chives

Make sure you've got
2 oranges
2 bananas
mayonnaise (1/2cup), bought or
    homemade, see page 87)

ahead
❶ Segment the oranges by peeling them completely, then cutting each segment free of its membrane: Do this over a bowl to catch the juice. Drop the segments into the bowl as you free them and squeeze any juice remaining in the membranes afterward with your hand.
❷ Peel the bananas and slice them at an angle into the orange juice. Stir them lightly to make sure they are completely coated.
❸ Slice the chicken into bite-size strips and add to the bowl with the green onions. Crumble in the bacon, then fold in the mayonnaise to coat everything. Chill for 1 to 2 hours.

at the last minute
❹ Transfer the contents of the bowl to a serving dish and sprinkle with the nuts and chives to serve.

make it your own You can also make this dish with cooked turkey. If you buy it from the delicatessen counter, ask them to slice it very thickly, preferably by hand, so it remains sufficiently chunky.

smoked chicken with red-pepper sauce

Serves 6 to 8 (perfect to multiply for larger numbers) ● **30 to 40 minutes to prepare, plus chilling**

Look for smoked chickens in good delicatessens—smoked chickens are good to keep in your freezer.

What you need

1 smoked chicken, about 2 pounds 10 ounces

2 ounces firm goat cheese

handful of fresh parsley

2 tablespoons chopped walnut pieces

for the dressing

2 ounces marinated or chargrilled red bell peppers

1/2 cup fromage blanc or sour cream

salt and pepper

to serve

5 ounces black grapes, halved and seeded, if necessary

ahead

❶ Skin the chicken and remove the flesh from the carcass, including the wings and legs.

❷ Put 4 ounces of the chicken (use the shredded scraps from wings and carcass rather than the breast meat) in a food processor and whiz with the goat cheese and parsley until smooth. Transfer to a bowl and stir in the walnuts. (This stops the walnuts getting obliterated while processing the other ingredients.)

❸ Season and pile onto a large square of plastic wrap. Roll up the plastic wrap to shape the mixture into a 4-inch link-sausage shape, packing it firmly together. Put in the refrigerator and leave for a couple hours, or up to a day.

❹ Up to 4 hours before you want to serve, slice the remaining chicken as neatly as possible and cover.

❺ Make the dressing by whizzing the peppers and fromage blanc or sour cream in a food processor until smooth. Check and adjust the seasoning.

at the last minute

❻ Remove the sliced chicken from the refrigerator. Arrange the chicken on a large serving plate and drizzle with the sauce. Unwrap the smoked-chicken-sausage-and-walnut mousse and cut into thick slices. Top the sliced chicken with the mousse and scatter with grapes.

make it your own **This looks classy on individual plates. Top the chicken and sauce with a single slice of the mousse, plus a scattering of grapes.**

smoked chicken with red-pepper sauce

chicken and walnut salad (simple)

Serves 2 (easily halved) ● 10 to 15 minutes to prepare

What you need

7 ounces cooked chicken breast, skinless
  and boneless, cut into strips

4 cherry tomatoes, quartered

1 green onion, chopped

$1/2$ cup chopped walnuts

1 tablespoon sour cream

small handful of fresh mint

Make sure you've got

olive oil (2 tablespoon)

wine vinegar (1 teaspoon)

Dijon mustard (1 teaspoon)

❶ Put the chicken, tomatoes, green onion and walnuts in a bowl and mix lightly.

❷ Make the dressing by whisking the oil with the vinegar, then whisking in the mustard and sour cream.

❸ Fold the salad and dressing together, and scatter thickly with the mint.

spicy chicken paprika

Serves 2 ● 10 to 20 minutes to prepare

What you need

$1/2$ cup fromage blanc, plus a little extra

$1 1/4$ ounces chargrilled or marinated peppers,
  sliced

1 celery stalk, chopped

7 ounces cooked chili-flavored chicken, sliced
  into bite-size pieces

2 ready-to-eat pappadams or a handful of
  tortilla chips

Make sure you've got

chutney (1 tablespoon)

smoked paprika ($1/2$ teaspoon)

squeeze of lemon juice, if you like

❶ Make the sauce by mixing 7 tablespoons fromage blanc with the peppers, chutney, celery, and paprika. The mixture should not need any extra seasoning. Stir in the sliced chicken.

❷ Pile on the pappadams or tortilla chips and top with extra fromage blanc. Some lemon juice adds zing.

Circassian chicken

Serves 4 (easily halved or multiplied) ● 10 to 20 minutes to prepare, plus chilling

In this traditional Turkish salad, chicken is smothered in a bread-and-walnut sauce.

What you need
4 cooked skinless and boneless chicken
    breast halves, each about $3^1/_2$ ounces
1 cup walnuts
freshly chopped tarragon, to finish (optional)

Make sure you've got
boiling water (1 cup)
good-quality vegetable bouillon granules,
    (1 teaspoon)
fresh white bread, crusts removed ($2^1/_2$ ounces)
walnut oil (1 tablespoon)
paprika ($^3/_4$ teaspoon)

ahead

❶ Cut each chicken breast at an angle across the grain into 5 or 6 slices, keeping the slices separate.

❷ In small bowl, pour the boiling water over the bouillon granules and mix well. Process the walnuts with the bread in a food processor and add enough of the bouillon mixture to make a sloppy paste.

❸ Reassemble each of the chicken breasts on a shallow serving dish or plate, slice by slice and with 1 teaspoon of the sauce between each slice. When all the breasts are reassembled, spoon the remaining sauce over to mask the chicken pieces completely. Chill for at least 30 minutes or up to 4 hours. Mix the walnut oil and paprika together and set aside.

at the last minute

❹ If any liquid has leaked from the sauce, blot it up with a paper towel. Drizzle with the red walnut oil and serve sprinkled with tarragon, if you wish.

Jubilee chicken (simple)

Serves 6 ● 20 to 30 minutes to prepare

Invented for Queen Elizabeth II's Golden Jubilee celebrations, this is a fresh take on coronation chicken, the curried chicken dish devised for her coronation.

What you need

6 cooked skinless and boneless chicken breast
    halves (about 1 pound 5 ounces)

12 ounces fresh cherries

6 ounces fresh watercress

4 to 5 green onions, shredded

1 cup fromage blanc

small handful of fresh mint, to finish

Make sure you've got

curry paste (1 tablespoon, see note on
    page 14)

honey (1 teaspoon)

½ lemon

salt and pepper

ahead

❶ Cut the chicken into bite-size pieces. Pit the cherries—or better still, get someone to do it for you.

❷ Layer up the ingredients in your serving dish: First the watercress, then the chicken, next the cherries, and finally the green onions.

at the last minute

❸ Make the dressing by whisking together the fromage blanc, curry paste, honey, and 1 tablespoon lemon juice. Season to taste and drizzle over the salad. Finally, sprinkle the salad with mint.

deviled chicken and avocado salad

Serves 4 (easily halved or doubled) ● **15 to 25 minutes preparation (depending on whether you've bought chicken already skinned and boned)**

What you need

7 tablespoons crème fraîche or sour cream

4 ounces young spinach leaves, rinsed, if necessary

1 pound cooked chicken (about $1/2$ medium roast
   chicken) on the bone, or $10^1/2$ ounces off

2 ripe tomatoes, white cores removed, cut into
   thin wedges, and seeds and pulp discarded

1 avocado, pitted, peeled, and cut into thin strips

Make sure you've got

1 garlic clove, crushed

Dijon mustard (2 teaspoons)

tomato catsup (2 teaspoons)

salt and pepper

Tabasco sauce (good splash of)

Worcestershire sauce (good splash of)

smoked paprika for dusting

ahead

❶ Make the dressing by whisking the crème fraîche, garlic, mustard, catsup, and sauces together. Adjust the seasoning, if necessary.

at the last minute

❷ Put the spinach in a large bowl, season, and toss with one-third of the dressing. Arrange on a serving dish. Add the remaining ingredients, except the paprika and the rest of the dressing, to the just-vacated bowl. Stir and toss them on top of the spinach. Dust with smoked paprika.

Hass avocados, often from South Africa, are the wrinkly, black-skinned ones. They have the advantage of not going brown, once cut, for up to 2 hours. The way to get the peel off is to halve them lengthwise and twist the halves to separate and remove the pit. Don't peel at this point—instead, slice the flesh or cut it in cubes (without cutting through the skin), then run a rubber spatula between flesh and skin and pop out the cubes of flesh.

Marsala chicken with golden raisins

Serves 4 ● 10 to 15 minutes to prepare (make 1 to 2 hours, or even up to a day, ahead)

This simple dish is elegant and understated.

What you need
2 tablespoons Marsala wine
4 cooked skinless and boneless chicken
    breast halves

Make sure you've got
golden raisins or seedless raisins (2 ounces)
$1/2$ orange (finely grated zest of)
boiling water
balsamic vinegar (2 teaspoons)
salt and pepper
olive oil (4 tablespoons)

ahead

❶ Put the golden raisins or seedless raisins (or raisins) and orange zest in a small bowl and pour enough boiling water to cover over. Leave to stand for at least 10 minutes and up to an hour. Drain, reserving the golden raisins and orange zest.

❷ Whisk the Marsala and vinegar with seasoning to taste and then whisk in the oil until blended into a sauce. Add the reserved raisins and orange zest.

❸ Slice the chicken neatly and thinly. Arrange on a serving dish and pour the sauce over. Leave at room temperature and then serve, or chill overnight. Bring back to room temperature to serve.

This needs a very plain accompaniment, such as couscous (page 99.) If also serving a salad, bring it out after the main course, as a vinegary dressing will spoil the sweetness of the sauce.

Balsamic vinegar varies: The oldest and best is slightly thick and very sweet; supermarket brands can be thin and more like soy sauce. If you have only the latter, taste carefully and add less balsamic vinegar, or extra sugar, as necessary.

make it your own
Instead of the Marsala wine, you can use sweet sherry, sweet white wine, or even dry white wine with $1/2$ teaspoon sugar dissolved in it. ● You can use lemon zest instead of orange. In the original Italian recipe, candied lemon peel is used, but I find this a bit too much like a fruit cake for modern tastes.

warm three-cheese salad *(simple)*

Serves 4 (easily halved or doubled) ● **10 to 15 minutes to prepare**

What you need

3½ ounces arugula leaves

2 ripe pears, peeled and each sliced into
    8 slim wedges and dipped in
    lemon juice

5 ounces good ripe Brie, cut into cubes

4 ounces firm goat cheese, cut into
    thin slices

½ cup roughly chopped walnuts

1 cup grated Double Gloucester or
    cheddar cheese

cress

Make sure you've got

salt and pepper

a squeeze of lemon juice

olive oil (2 tablespoons)

walnut oil (2 tablespoons)

sherry vinegar, red-wine vinegar, or
    balsamic vinegar (2 teaspoons)

ahead

❶ Layer up the salad in a large bowl, seasoning lightly with a little salt and plenty of black pepper as you go. Start with the arugula, then the pear slices, followed by the Brie and the goat cheese. Scatter with walnuts and the grated cheese, then snip over the cress.

at the last minute

❷ Heat the oils and vinegar in a microwave or small pan until boiling. Whisk together and pour over the salad. Toss and serve at once.

make it your own
This salad can be infinitely varied. The essential components are a soft cheese, a semisoft cheese, and a firm cheese in any combination. If you are an Anglophile, go for a British Brie, an English goat cheese, and any of the fine English hard cheeses. For an Italian taste, use Dolcelatte, Taleggio, and Parmesan for grating. Spend some time sampling new cheeses at a good cheese store that imports.

Eastern supper

Serves 4—easily halved or doubled ● 20 to 30 minutes to prepare

This feast of lovely dishes—only one of which needs cooking—is the equivalent of a vegetarian curry supper and gives an engaging banquet feeling.

What you need

for the peach relish
2 fresh peaches
1-inch piece fresh root ginger, peeled and
    finely chopped
4 green onions, shredded

for the cilantro yoghurt
$^2/_3$cup thick plain yogurt
handful of cilantro, chopped
juice of $^1/_2$ lime

for the couscous
squeeze of lime juice

for the vegetables
14 ounces antipasto vegetables—red bell
    peppers, eggplants, artichokes, sun-dried
    tomatoes, olives, all sliced or roughly
    chopped

Make sure you've got
red-wine vinegar (2 teaspoons)
salt
quick-cook couscous (1 $^1/_2$cups)
olive oil (1 tablespoon)
curry paste (1 tablespoon)
1 cup boiling water

❶ Make the peach relish: Score the peach skins into quarters, pour boiling water to cover generously over, and, after 30 seconds, lift out with a fork and remove the skins. Chop the flesh and stir together with the ginger, green onions and vinegar.

❷ Make the cilantro yogurt by mixing all the ingredients together, adding a pinch of salt.

❸ Make the couscous by putting it into a heatproof bowl with the olive oil. Put the curry paste into a measuring jug, stir in the boiling water, and pour over the couscous. Add the lime juice and leave for 10 minutes, stirring occasionally.

❹ Prepare the vegetables by piling them into a strainer and rinsing them under cold running water.

❺ To serve, stir the vegetables into the couscous and serve with the accompaniments.

a shopping hint Check out the small print on your curry paste—some brands need to be cooked to use. If that is the case, stir-fry it for a minute or two, or sizzle it in a small dish in the microwave, covered with plastic wrap.

make it your own For a more substantial feast (for meat eaters), add to the mêlée curried cooked chicken or turkey meat. Look for it at the deli counter.

Eastern supper

stylish
side dishes

save valuable time with imaginative no-cook accompaniments;
some refreshing, some unusual, but all inspired and certain
to complement the range of no-cook main courses

endive in the Belgian style

Serves 2 (easily multiplied) ● 10 to 20 minutes to prepare

What you need

½ ounce (4 little squares) white chocolate

4 teaspoons beer or lager, ideally Belgian

snipped fresh chives, to garnish

2 heads of Belgian endive, trimmed, cored,
   and cut into bite-size chunks

Make sure you've got

olive oil (4 teaspoons)

Dijon mustard (1 teaspoon)

salt and pepper

❶ Deal with the endive at the last minute, because it turns brown immediately.
❷ Melt the chocolate in the microwave or over hot water, then whisk in the beer until smooth. While still whisking, add the oil, mustard, and seasoning.
❸ Drizzle this over the endive and scatter with snipped chives. Serve.

real Greek salad (simple)

Serves 4 (easily halved or doubled) ● 10 to 20 minutes to prepare

What you need

4 large tomatoes, seeds and pulp discarded, diced

2½-inch piece of cucumber, peeled, seeded,
   and diced

2 celery stalks, diced

1 yellow bell pepper, seeded and diced

12 to 16 green, red, or black olives, pitted and
   roughly chopped

2 green onions, shredded

9 ounces feta in oil, cut into ½-inch cubes

handful of fresh mint, chopped

Make sure you've got

extra-virgin olive oil (4 tablespoons)

lemon juice (4 teaspoons)

salt and pepper

❶ Mix together all the vegetables, along with the cheese and mint.
❷ Mix the oil and lemon juice to make a dressing and fold it into the salad. Season to taste. Serve at once or chill, and then bring back to room temperature to serve.

Vietnamese coleslaw

Serves 4 ● 15 to 20 minutes to prepare

Here, unusual flavors take coleslaw to new heights.

What you need
3 green onions
½ small white cabbage
1 large carrot
a couple of celery stalks, or 1 fennel bulb
⅓ cup salted peanuts (not dry-roasted)

Make sure you've got
1 small red chili
peanut butter (2 tablespoons)
mayonnaise (4 tablespoons)
soy sauce (good splash)

ahead
❶ Shred the green onions and seed and finely chop the chilli. Very thinly slice the cabbage, carrot, and celery, either on a grater, in a food processor, or by hand. Mix all these ingredients together in a big bowl.
❷ In a small bowl, whisk together the peanut butter, mayo, and soy sauce. Fold this dressing into the coleslaw. No added salt and pepper are necessary.
❸ Sprinkle with the peanuts and serve.

make it your own You can build this into more of a main course by adding one or two skinned and shredded cooked chicken breasts. Vegetarians can add Quorn or tofu, sliced into strips. Rice crackers make a nice accompaniment.

dressing to impress

When making salad dressings, there are many tempting oils and vinegars to choose from. Olive oil and extra-virgin olive oil are, of course, the automatic choice for Mediterranean-type dishes, but otherwise I use sunflower. New-kid-on-the-block argan oil, from Morocco, is nutty and mild, with an attractive greenish hue. Nut oils (especially sesame) are best used with equal parts sunflower as they are strong (in the case of dark sesame oil, a few drops will do). Some flavored vinegars are sweet, especially fruit and flower ones, and you do not need to add extra sugar. Rice-wine vinegar is great for Oriental-type salads. If I want a lemony taste, I usually add a little finely grated zest or a very little juice, as too much juice cam make a dressing acid.

1 make your own mayo Bought mayonnaise is great, but home-made is even better. I don't use olive oil as this tastes bitter. For classic mayonnaise, put 2 or 3 egg yolks, 4 teaspoons Dijon mustard, a squeeze of lemon juice, and some seasoning in a blender or processor. Start adding 1/4–2cups sunflower oil, drop by drop, gradually increasing the quantity until you are adding it in a thin stream. Taste and stop adding oil when the eggy taste is gone, but before the mayo starts to taste oily. I add 1 to 3 tablespoons boiling water at this point to make the texture more light and whippy.

2 cheat's mayo It's not exactly cheating, but you can make brilliant mayo with a stick blender and the tall, narrow jug that comes with it. Put 1 whole egg, 2/3cup sunflower oil, 4 teaspoons Dijon mustard, salt, pepper, and a squeeze of lemon juice in the jug. Put the blender right to the bottom, over the egg, and switch on. After a few seconds, very slowly start to lift the stick blender. Hey presto!

3 avocado-aise Make a lighter, fresher mayonnaise by processing 1 egg yolk, the flesh of 1/2 avocado, mustard, lemon juice, and seasoning, with 2/3 to 1 1/4cups sunflower oil in the same way as classic mayonnaise above.

4 season your salad, not your dressing With a leaf salad, put the salt and pepper on the leaves, not in the dressing. Lightly tumble the leaves about in the salad bowl with the seasoning, then add the dressing.

5 give yourself some space Don't try and toss your salad in too small a bowl—either you won't do the job properly or the salad will go everywhere (or both). If your serving bowl is small, toss the salad in a big bowl, then transfer to the serving bowl. If there are only two of you and you are using a bagged salad, put the dressing in the bag and lightly shake, then transfer directly to plates.

6 whisking is the secret One secret of a great dressing is to emulsify the oil and vinegar well, as this blends the flavors and gives a silky coating to salad ingredients. Using a microwhisk or mini-balloon whisk is better than a fork or shaking the ingredients in a jar.

7 sea salt and freshly ground black pepper Grind your own sea salt—English Maldon salt, or the French fleur de sel—using a mortar and pestle, and add by the pinch. The flavor is finer and cleaner. Always grind black peppercorns fresh, and, for more impact, add a pinch of crushed chilies.

8 good for you Salads that include citrus fruit, such as grapefruit, might not need any dressing at all—let the juice do the work. If using lemon juice in a dressing, remember that too much can make it acid—boost the lemon flavor with some finely grated zest. Rice-wine vinegar is mild enough to be used without oil. Whisk flavorings into fromage blanc for a creamy dressing without fat.

9 the winning formula Everyone's taste differs, but I use 3 tablespoons oil to 2 teaspoons vinegar for a salad for 3 or 4 people. I usually add 1 to 2 teaspoons Dijon mustard and a pinch of sugar, and simply put everything into a small bowl and whisk until combined.

10 dressing too strong? If you generally find dressings too strong, you can use a French trick: Whisk 1 tablespoon water into a vinaigrette dressing. This slows the speed at which the vinegar hits the palate, and rounds out the flavor without diluting it.

LEFT give yourself some space

BELOW sea salt and freshly ground black pepper

ABOVE whisking is the secret

RIGHT good for you

a trio of Moroccan salads *(simple)*

These are all best served at room temperature, accompanied by flat breads ● Each salad serves 2, but if you make all three you will have enough for 4 to 6 ● Tomato and beet salads take 5 to 10 minutes to prepare, the carrot 15 to 20 minutes

tomato and lemon

What you need

2 ripe, juicy medium-size tomatoes

1 miniature preserved lemon, seeds removed
    and very thinly sliced

Make sure you've got

ground cumin ($\frac{1}{2}$ teaspoon)

extra-virgin olive oil or argan oil (1 tablespoon)

salt and pepper

sugar

❶ Halve the tomatoes and discard their seeds and pulp. Slice them thinly.

❷ Mix with the cumin, preserved lemon, oil, plenty of seasoning, and a pinch of sugar.

beets and rosewater

What you need

4 ounces cooked baby beets

Make sure you've got

rosewater (1 tablespoon)

extra-virgin olive oil or argan oil (1 tablespoon)

❶ Cut each beet into 6 tiny wedges. Mix with the rosewater and oil, and season well.

carrot and harissa

What you need

2 carrots, peeled

Make sure you've got

boiling water

harissa paste (1 teaspoon)

extra-virgin olive oil or argan oil (2 teaspoons)

salt and pepper

$\frac{1}{2}$ lemon

❶ Cut the carrots into matchsticks as small as patience will allow. Put these in a heatproof bowl. Pour boiling water to cover over and leave for 5 minutes; drain and refresh in cold water. Drain again and pat dry with paper towels.

❷ Mix with the harissa, oil, and plenty of salt and pepper. Squeeze lemon juice over just before serving.

succotash salad (simple)

Serves 4 to 6 ● 10 to 20 minutes to prepare, plus chilling

This colorful jumble is fresh goodness. Use the can the corn comes in as a measure for the other ingredients.

What you need

10-ounce can of corn kernels, drained

1 canful of frozen fava beans

1 canful of finely diced zucchini (1 small zucchini)

1/2 canful of finely diced cucumber

1 canful of seeded tomatoes (about 3 medium tomatoes), cut into strips

2 green onions, shredded

2 large slices of chargrilled bell pepper (such as Spanish piquillo), sliced

10 fresh mint leaves, finely chopped

Make sure you've got

boiling water

salt and pepper

1 garlic clove, crushed

sunflower oil (2 tablespoons)

white-wine vinegar (2 teaspoons)

ahead

❶ Empty the corn into a big bowl, and use the can to measure the beans and zucchini into another bowl. Pour boiling water over the vegetables and leave for 5 minutes to blanch, then drain.

❷ Mix the blanched vegetables into the corn, together with the cucumber, tomatoes, green onions and pepper; season well.

❸ Make the dressing by mixing (either by hand or in a processor) the garlic, mint, oil, and vinegar. Pour it over the salad and chill until ready to serve.

at the last minute

❹ Adjust the seasoning, if necessary. If the salad has been standing for more than a few minutes, transfer with a slotted spoon to a fresh bowl, leaving behind the juices.

This is a great salad for a party. Scale it up for eight by using a large can of corn, or multiply.

pear, beet, and Stilton salad (simple)

Serves 4 as a side dish or appetizer (easily halved) ● 10 to 15 minutes to prepare

What you need

2 pears, peeled and each sliced into 8 wedges

8 ounces cooked beets, sliced into 8 wedges

4 ounces Stilton cheese, cut into small cubes

7 tablespoons crème fraîche

Make sure you've got

balsamic vinegar (1 teaspoon)

pepper

ahead

❶ On a shallow serving dish, fan out alternating pear and beet wedges.

❷ Lightly mix together the Stilton, crème fraîche, and vinegar.

at the last minute

❸ Season the pears and beet with pepper and drizzle the sauce over them. Toss together and serve.

orange three-bean salad (simple)

Serves 4 (easily halved or doubled) ● 10 to 20 minutes to prepare

What you need

8 ounces frozen fava beans

14-ounce can of garbanzo beans, rinsed and
    drained

14-ounce can of black beans, rinsed and
    drained

snipped fresh chives or chopped fresh parsley,
    to finish

Make sure you've got

salt ($1/2$ teaspoon)

boiling water

rice-wine vinegar (4 teaspoons)

finely grated zest of $1/2$ orange and 4 teaspoons juice

freshly grated root ginger (2 teaspoons)

sunflower oil (5 tablespoons)

toasted sunflower oil (few drops, optional)

❶ Put the fava beans in a bowl with the salt, pour lots of boiling water over, and leave for 5 to 10 minutes. Drain, put back in the bowl, cover with cold water to chill quickly, then drain again. Mix with the garbanzo beans and black beans.

❷ Mix together all the remaining ingredients, except the herbs. Mix into the beans, then fold in the herbs.

lentil and radish salad (simple)

Serves 4 ● 10 to 15 minutes to prepare

What you need
16 radishes
big handful of fresh parsley
14-ounce can of green or brown lentils,
    rinsed and drained

Make sure you've got
caraway seeds (1 tablespoon)
2 garlic cloves, finely chopped
sherry vinegar (1 tablespoon)
wholegrain mustard (3 tablespoons)
salt and pepper
extra-virgin olive oil (5 tablespoons)

ahead

❶ Roughly crush the caraway seeds using a mortar and pestle . If you've got a large one, add the garlic and mash that too—and make the dressing in the mortar. Otherwise, make the dressing in a bowl.

❷ Whisk in the vinegar, mustard, and seasoning, followed by the oil, to make a dressing.

at the last minute

❸ Roughly chop the radishes and finely chop the parsley. Fold these into the lentils with the dressing.

cucumber with poppy seeds (simple)

Serves 4 ● 5 to 10 minutes to prepare

What you need
1 small cucumber (about 14ounces)

Make sure you've got
1/2 red chili, very finely chopped
poppy seeds (2 teaspoons)
rice-wine vinegar (1 1/2 teaspoons)

❶ Peel the cucumber and halve it down the middle. Drag a spoon down the middle to scrape away the seeds and discard them. Slice the cucumber crosswise into crescents and put in a serving bowl.

❷ Scatter the chili, poppy seeds, and vinegar over. Serve.

tomato tabbouleh

Serves 6 ● 15 to 20 minutes to prepare (thanks to the food processor), plus overnight chilling

What you need

1 1/3 cups bulgar wheat (not the coarse kind)

large handful of fresh parsley

small handful of fresh mint

1 large carrot, peeled and quartered

1 large green bell pepper, quartered

1 1/4 cups V8 vegetable juice

Make sure you've got

1 onion

1 lemon (juice of)

extra-virgin olive oil (3 tablespoons)

salt

ahead
❶ Bulgar wheat can need rinsing; if in doubt, rinse it in a strainer. Tip it into a large bowl.
❷ Chop the herbs finely and add to the bulgar. Do the same with each vegetable.
❸ Stir in the remaining ingredients with 7 ounces water and 1/2 teaspoon salt, and leave in the refrigerator overnight.

at the last minute
❹ Bring to room temperature and drain any unabsorbed liquid before serving.

jeweled couscous

Serves 2 (easily doubled) ● 10 to 20 minutes to prepare

What you need

2/3 cup couscous

1 tablespoon dried cranberries

2 fresh dates, finely chopped

1 fresh apricot, finely chopped

fresh cilantro leaves, chopped

Make sure you've got

good-quality vegetable bouillon granules
   (1 teaspoon)

olive oil (1 tablespoon, optional)

boiling water (7 ounces)

salt and pepper

❶ Put the couscous in a bowl with the bouillon granules, cranberries, and oil, if using.
❷ Pour the boiling water over and leave for 10 minutes, stirring occasionally.
❸ Stir in the fresh fruit. Add the cilantro and season. Fluff again to serve.

something on the side

To fill that potato-shaped space, instead of buying expensive—and not always very nice— potato salads and the like, try some of these wonderfully nutty, healthy grains or satisfying noodles that only require soaking in boiling water.

COUSCOUS This North African staple is a cupboard must. Put 1^1/$_2$cups in a bowl, cover with 2cups boiling water with some seasoning, and leave for a minimum of 10 minutes, stirring occasionally with a fork. Finely grated lemon or lime zest and juice, freshly grated gingerroot, soy sauce, and other flavorings can be added with the water. Chopped herbs can be forked in just before serving.

herby lemon couscous Plain couscous is a good foil for other flavors, but I usually add 1^1/$_2$ teaspoons good-quality vegetable bouillon granules, in place of seasoning, the juice of ^{1}/$_2$ lemon, and 1 tablespoon extra-virgin olive (or a flavored) oil. Finish by forking in freshly chopped mint, cilantro, or parsley.

tabbouleh To make this classic Arabian salad for 4 to 6, put 1cup bulgar wheat in a bowl and mix with the juice of a lemon, plenty of salt, pepper, a pinch of cayenne, a chopped tomato, 2 shredded green onions, 2 tablespoons olive oil, and a large handful each of parsley and mint (the volume of chopped herbs should be greater than the volume of bulgar). Pour 2cups water over and leave for 30 minutes. Squeeze out any excess liquid, adjust the seasoning, and serve.

bulgar wheat Not found in every supermarket, but you'll get it in health-food stores. For no-cooking, you need finely ground bulgar, not coarse (if not specified, it's likely to be fine). Simply add water (quantity isn't critical, but I use 1cup bulgar to 2cups liquid) and leave for at least 30 minutes for the grain to swell. Squeeze out excess liquid. Lots of herbs, flavorings, and seasoning are called for—add with the water.

barley couscous One up on plain couscous, this has more flavor, a slightly darker color, and a slightly more chewy consistency. Make it in just the same way.

6 Chinese egg noodles Usually sold as "instant noodles," these are indispensable for no-cooking. They have a good firm consistency and are already seasoned, so they enhance most dishes. Avoid flavored varieties, which have an artificial taste. Package directions usually tell you to boil them for 2 minutes, but I get perfect results by putting them in a heatproof bowl (do not add salt) and covering with boiling water. Leave for 10 minutes, stirring occasionally. Check they're tender; if not, leave a little longer. If you're going to incorporate the noodles into other ingredients, break them up a bit before adding the boiling water—this makes them less tangly and easier to mix in.

7 savory noodles To serve noodles as a side dish, splash soy, sweet chili sauce, or teriyaki sauce over Chinese egg noodles.

8 rice noodles As fast and convenient as Chinese egg noodles, these are more suited to delicate Thai flavors. Sprinkle $1/2$ teaspoon salt over the noodles in a heatproof bowl, cover with boiling water, and leave for 4 to 6 minutes, or according to the package directions. Don't prepare until you need them, or they stick together. These noodles are also inclined to tangle, so if they are to be mixed with other ingredients snap them into pieces before you soak them.

9 Thai stir-fry noodles Also known as stick noodles or rice sticks, these come in tiny sheaves, a bit like doll's-house spaghetti. As with the broader rice noodles, leave these in salted boiling water for 4 minutes, and don't make ahead. When combining with other ingredients, fold in a few at a time or layer

10 vermicelli This most light and delicate member of the pasta family doesn't need cooking. Treat like oriental noodles—put in a bowl with salt and cover with boiling water. After 10 minutes, drain and use. Vermicelli will break up if you mix it with other ingredients, so layer it instead.

LEFT fine rice noodles or rice sticks

BELOW dried egg noodles soaking in boiling water

RIGHT broad rice noodles or rice sticks

FAR RIGHT nests of fine egg noodles

as long as it is balanced, no-cooking can, by its very nature, be incredibly good for you, as it relies so heavily on nutritious raw vegetables and fruit. If you are counting carbs and fat, these recipes have nutritional analyses

deliciously healthy

fruits-of-the-forest thickie *(simple)*

Serves 2 (or 2 indulgent drinks for one deserving person) ● 5 minutes to prepare

What you need

9 ounces mixed frozen fruits of the forest
   (wild berry fruit)

1 banana

1¼ to 2 cups plain yogurt

Make sure you've got

honey or maple syrup (2 to 3 teaspoons)

❶ Whiz the still-frozen fruits of the forest in a food processor until finely chopped.
❷ Add the banana and whiz again. Scrape down the side, then add the honey or syrup and enough yogurt to make your preferred sweetness and consistency. It is impossible to be too dogmatic, as fruit and yogurt vary so much.
❸ Transvase into long glasses and drink in the health.

make it your own The formula is identical for other fruit drinks. Put in the main fruit (fresh or frozen) before the other ingredients and make sure it is thoroughly blitzed. ● Strawberries, raspberries, blackberries, blueberries, mango, and pineapple are all good for healthy drinks. Or use a mixture of two—not more than two, or the taste will be lost. ● Follow your taste buds and add a sprig of mint at step 1, or 3 drops vanilla extract. If it is too thick for your taste, dilute it with orange or apple juice. ● On a really hot day, make ice cubes out of fruit juice and use to cool the thickies.

per serving Energy 166 calories, protein 9. 2g, carbohydrate 30. 2g, fat 1. 8g, saturated fat 1. 0g, fiber 3. 6g, added sugars none, salt 0. 33g ● Super healthy; good source of calcium and vitamin C; very low in calories and fat; counts as 2 fruit servings on the Food Pyramid.

avocado and grapefruit salad

Serves 2 ● 10 to 15 minutes to prepare

Think California here for this beautiful fresh zingy salad of enormous delicacy, inspired by chef Alice Waters. It is enough to convert the most confirmed grapefruit hater.

What you need
2 medium-size pink grapefruits
4 green onions, shredded
small bag of arugula
1 ripe avocado, pitted, peeled, and cut into
    thin slices
fresh chives, to snip over

Make sure you've got
wine-vinegar or sherry vinegar (2 teaspoons)
extra-virgin olive oil (5 tablespoons)

❶ Segment the grapefruit as described below. Put the segments in a bowl and squeeze the juice from the membranes and pith over. Lift out the segments and mix with the green onions.
❷ Remove 1 tablespoon of the grapefruit juice (drink or save the rest) and put in a small bowl. Whisk with the vinegar, oil, and seasoning.
❸ Toss the arugula lightly with 1 tablespoon of this dressing and arrange on 2 plates.
❹ Top with the grapefruit and avocado and drizzle the dressing over. Snip chives over.

If you've never segmented an orange or grapefruit, it's a trick worth knowing as the fruit is so delicious prepared this way. First get your knife good and sharp. Peel off all the skin and pith with the knife, then slice each individual segment free of its membrane, so it pops out easily, gradually leaving a fan of the tough membranes. Do this over a bowl to catch the juice.

per serving Energy 400 kcalories, protein 4.6g, carbohydrate 15.1g, fat 36.0g, saturated fat 4.7g, fiber 5.7g, added sugars none, salt 0.04g. ● Super healthy; although high in overall fat content because of the avocado and the oil, low in saturated fat and salt; good source of folic acid and vitamin C; counts as 2 fruit servings on the Food Pyramid.

chicken with pink grapefruit and corn

Serves 2 ● 20 to 25 minutes to prepare

This salad is light, pretty, and deliciously fresh.

What you need

8 ounces cooked chicken, skinless and
    boneless

1 corn on the cob, or a 10-ounce can of corn
    kernels, drained

1 pink grapefruit

Make sure you've got

boiling water

½ red chili

salt and pepper

❶ Slice the chicken and put it in a bowl.

❷ Strip the kernels off the cob into another bowl. (Stand the cob on end and cut right down with a heavy knife at several points all around.) Pour boiling water over and leave for 5 minutes, then drain and add to the chicken. If using canned, just drain.

❸ Peel the grapefruit with a knife and segment it as described on page 105, holding it in your hand and rotating it as you go. Add the segments to the chicken. Using your hand, squeeze the juice from the membranes over the chicken and discard them.

❹ Seed the chili and chop it finely, then stir it into the other ingredients and season the salad well. The salad can be eaten at once or chilled. Simple couscous (page 99) makes a good accompaniment.

per serving Energy 201 calories, protein 27.2g, carbohydrate 18.5g, fat 2.4g, saturated fat 0.4g, fiber 2.3g, added sugars none, salt 0.16g. ● Super healthy; very low in fat and added sugars; good source of folic acid and vitamin C; counts as a fruit and a vegetable serving on the Food Pyramid.

chunky fresh tomato soup

Serves 6 (serve with bread for a main course) ● 10 to 20 minutes to prepare, plus chilling

Use the best ripe tomatoes you can find. Out of season, it helps to add a dash of tomato paste to improve the color of the soup.

What you need

8 juicy, ripe medium-size tomatoes

1 small red onion, roughly chopped

good handful of fresh cilantro, plus extra to serve

2$\frac{1}{4}$cups passata (crushed tomatoes—look for jars at
    Italian delis)

14-ounce can of cannellini beans, drained

tortilla chips, to serve

❶ Halve the tomatoes and squeeze out the seeds and pulp. Put the flesh in a food processor with the onion and cilantro and whiz until chopped.

❷ Transfer to a bowl and stir in the passata, beans, and seasoning, plus $\frac{2}{3}$cup cold water.

❸ Serve well chilled, with more cilantro and tortilla chips.

make it your own You can use dry white wine instead of water in Step 2. ● You can top the soup with a spoonful of homemade pesto: Process a large handful of basil (or another herb) with 2 tablespoons pine nuts, 1 ounce Parmesan cheese, 1 garlic clove, and 3 tablespoons olive oil. Add a splash of water if it is too thick to spoon.

per serving

Energy 92 calories, protein 5.1g, carbohydrate 16.8g, fat 1.0g, saturated fat 0.1g, fiber 3.7g, added sugars 1.3g, salt 0.56g ● Super healthy; very low in calories and fat; good source of vitamin C; counts as 2 vegetable servings on the Food Pyramid. Tomatoes (fresh, canned, and cooked) are rich in lycopenes, which help prevent heart disease and cancer.

fresh pea soup *(simple)*

Serves 4 ● 10 to 20 minutes to prepare

This soup is deceptively simple, but never fails to surprise with its satisfying full flavor. Frozen peas manage to keep a lot of their taste, but the fresh mint and chives make all the difference.

What you need
1 pound frozen shelled peas
generous handful of mint
4 tablespoons heavy (whipping) cream
a few fresh chives

Make sure you've got
boiling water
good-quality vegetable bouillon granules
   (1 tablespoon)

❶ Measure $3^3/_4$ cups boiling water into a jug and add the bouillon granules and peas.
❷ Leave for at least 10 minutes, or until cool, then puree the peas and liquid with the mint in a blender or food processor until completely smooth: This will take a couple of minutes.
❸ Chill and serve with a swirl of cream and snipped chives on top.

A blender makes a smoother soup than a food processor.

per serving Energy 152 calories, protein 7.1g, carbohydrate 12.0g, fat 8.7g, saturated fat 4.9g, fiber 5.8g, added sugars none, salt 0.19g ● Super healthy; low in saturated fat; counts as 1 vegetable serving on the Food Pyramid.

ABOVE chunky fresh tomato soup RIGHT fresh pea soup

panzanella (simple)

Serves 2 ● 10 to 20 minutes to prepare (best left to sit for 30 minutes before eating)

The Tuscans don't like wasting bread, and when it begins to get stale, they use it in a thick tomato soup (*pappa*), as well as this Tuscan bread salad.

What you need
4 ounces cucumber (3½ to 4 inches)
1 small red onion, very thinly sliced, or
    2 green onions, shredded
12 to 15 cherry tomatoes, halved
about 2 ounces fresh basil leaves
3 ounces day-old ciabatta

Make sure you've got
salt
extra-virgin olive oil (3 tablespoons)
red-wine vinegar (1 tablespoon)

❶ Partly peel the cucumber with a potato peeler so it is striped. Slice down the middle and scrape out the seeds and pulp. Cut across into thin slices and put in a strainer or colander with the red onion or green onions. Sprinkle with 1 teaspoon salt and mix; leave to drain.

❷ Squeeze the seeds and pulp out of the tomatoes and discard. Put the tomatoes in a serving bowl with the basil.

❸ Tear the bread (crusts and all) into bite-size chunks and put them into a bowl of water. Immediately lift out handfuls and squeeze them dry (not so firmly they are squashed, but enough that they are spongy) and transfer to the bowl with the tomatoes. Mix together and leave for about 30 minutes.

❹ Pat the cucumber and onion dry with paper towels and mix with the bread and tomato.

❺ Whisk the oil and vinegar to make a dressing and toss together with the salad. The salad should not need extra salt.

Dissertations have been written on what bread to use for panzanella, how stale it should be, exactly how hard to squeeze it out. I think, though, that the important thing is to use coarse country bread, and aim for the finished effect to be damp, light, and fluffy.

make it your own This is meant to be a simple salad, but Tuscans sometimes add sliced anchovy fillets or chargrilled peppers, cut into strips, with the tomatoes. I like to add sliced mozzarella at the end.

per serving Energy 257 calories, protein 3.6g, carbohydrate 21.1g, fat 17.8g, saturated fat 2.6g, fiber 1.8g, added sugars none, salt 0.71g ● Super healthy; low in saturated fat; counts as 1 vegetable serving on the Food Pyramid.

panzanella

shrimp and avocado escabèche

Serves 2 ● 10 to 15 minutes to prepare (start the day before, if convenient)

An escabèche is a cold dish of cooked fish in a sweet-and-sour marinade, often including chili and vinegar—or, as here, lime juice.

What you need
juice of 1 lime
4 green onions, shredded
7 ounces cherry or plum tomatoes, pulp
    and seeds discarded, chopped
4 ounces shelled cooked shrimp, thawed
    if frozen
1 ripe avocado, pitted, peeled, and cubed
small handful of chopped fresh cilantro

to serve
romain lettuce leaves
ready-to-eat pappadams or tortilla chips

Make sure you've got
tomato paste (2 teaspoons)
pinch of dried oregano
1 green chili, seeded and finely chopped

❶ Mix the lime juice, green onions, tomato paste, oregano, tomatoes, and chili in a non-metallic bowl. (You can refrigerate this marinade, covered with plastic wrap, for up to 3 days.)
❷ Stir in the shrimp, avocado, and cilantro, and leave for at least 10 minutes and up to 1 hour for the flavors to mingle.
❸ Arrange the lettuce leaves on plates and spoon the escabèche onto the leaves. Serve accompanied with pappadams or tortilla chips.

make it your own Use another cooked fish, such as salmon; buy a slightly larger quantity and flake it in.

per serving Energy 218 calories, protein 16.7g, carbohydrate 5.1g, fat 14.7g, saturated fat 1.7g, fiber 3.6g, added sugars none, salt 1.32g ● Super healthy; low in saturated fat; counts as 2 vegetable servings on the Food Pyramid.

smoked mackerel and horseradish salad

Per person ● 5 to 10 minutes to prepare

The pungency of horseradish is a classic foil for the oiliness of mackerel. The potato chips give the salad a welcome crunch.

What you need

1 smoked mackerel fillet (about 3 ounces)

4 ounces crisp lettuce leaves

1 green onion, shredded

1 ripe tomato, quartered, seeds and pulp
   discarded, then sliced

handful of potato chips

Make sure you've got

grated horseradish or horseradish sauce
   ($^1/_2$ teaspoon)

white-wine vinegar (1 teaspoon)

olive or sunflower oil (1 tablespoon)

salt and pepper

❶ Make the dressing by whisking together the horseradish, vinegar, and oil.

❷ Flake the fish and shred the lettuce into a bowl. Scatter the green onion and tomato over.

❸ Season the salad lightly (if the mackerel is peppered, you might not need any at all) and toss in the dressing. Scatter the potato chips over and enjoy.

make it your own **This is also good made with smoked trout fillets, or flaky hot-smoked salmon. In this case, use mustard instead of the horseradish.**

per serving **Energy 485 calories, protein 18.2g, carbohydrate 10.0g, fat 41.6g, saturated fat 9.2g, fiber 2.2g, added sugars none, salt 1.92g ● Good source of omega-3 fatty acids, folic acid and vitamin C; counts as 2 vegetable servings on the Food Pyramid.**

Thai shrimp with lime noodles

Serves 4 ● 15 to 20 minutes to prepare (stays good for 24 hours)

Although this is not authentically oriental, it is very easy and low in fat.

What you need

7 ounces sugar-snap peas, halved at an angle

7 ounces shelled cooked shrimp, thawed if frozen

7-ounce can of corn kernels, drained

4 green onions, shredded

handful of fresh cilantro, chopped

2 limes, finely grated zest and juice of 1, the
   other cut into 4 wedges, to serve

Make sure you've got

salt

boiling water

flat rice noodles (5 ounces)

Thai sweet chili sauce (1 tablespoon)

Thai fish sauce (nam pla) (1 tablespoon)

❶ Put the sugar-snap peas in a bowl with a little salt, pour boiling water over, and leave for 5 minutes to blanch; drain.

❷ Do the same with the noodles.

❸ Meanwhile, mix the shrimp, corn, and green onions in a serving bowl.

❹ Whisk the sauces with the lime zest and juice and add to the bowl along with the drained noodles.

❺ Stir in the cilantro and serve with lime quarters.

Flat rice noodles are so easy—put on the timer so you don't forget about them.

make it your own You can use 1 cup frozen peas instead of the sugar snaps—blanch them in exactly the same way.

per serving Energy 246 calories, protein 16.5g, carbohydrate 45.1g, fat 1.2, saturated fat 0.2g, fiber 1.5g, added sugars 3.2g, salt 2.24g ● Very low in fat and saturated fat; counts as 1 vegetable serving on the Food Pyramid.

tuna and cannellini bean salad *(simple)*

Serves 4 ● **10 minutes to prepare**

What you need
14-ounce can of cannellini beans, rinsed and
    drained
small handful of fresh mint, freshly chopped

Make sure you've got
5ounces canned tuna in oil, drained and flaked
1 small red onion, chopped
juice of 1/2 lemon

❶ Simply mix together all the ingredients and eat.

per serving Energy 130 calories, protein 13.3g, carbohydrate 12.5g, fat 3.4g, saturated fat 0.5g, fiber3.5g, added sugars none, salt 0.39g ● Super-healthy; low in calories, fat and saturated fat; counts as 1 vegetable serving on the Food Pyramid.

tomato and shrimp salad *(simple)*

per person ● **10 minutes to prepare**

What you need
4ounces shelled cooked jumbo shrimp
1 large tomato, seeds and pulps discarded,
    sliced into pieces the same size as the
    shrimp
chopped fresh cilantro

Make sure you've got
flat rice noodles (1 1/2ounces)
boiling water
olive oil (1 tablespoon)

❶ Snap the noodles into thirds, put into a bowl, and pour boiling water over them. Add 1teaspoon salt and leave for 4 minutes.
❷ Meanwhile, mix together all the other ingredients in a bowl.
❸ Drain the noodles, stir into the contents of the bowl, and eat.

per serving Energy 352 calories, protein 27.5g, carbohydrate 29.8g, fat 14.4g, saturated fat 1.7g, fiber 2.0g, added sugars none, salt 2.06g ● Low in saturated fat; good source of vitamin C; counts as 1 vegetable serving on the Food Pyramid.

trio of salsas

These classic Latin condiments make great accompaniments to bread, cheese, meat, or fish, adding kick, freshness, and lots of vitamins. The possibilities are endless, but your main ingredients should be diced rather than sliced, the consistency should be sloppy—and a salsa needs plenty of onion. Always mix them in a non-metallic bowl (to avoid a metallic taint) and chill well. Literally "raw sauce," salsa cruda is an excellent all-purpose juicy and chunky salsa, enough to serve with bread as an appetizer. For salsa verde, "green salsa," cut everything fairly finely to make a sort of relish that is especially useful in cooling down spicy-hot dishes, or to serve with fish. Sweet, juicy, crunchy salsa rosso is great with meats and barbecues.

salsa cruda (simple)

Serves 6 (can be halved) ● 10 minutes to prepare, plus chilling

What you need

2 orange, yellow, or red bell peppers, seeded and roughly chopped

6 small tomatoes, halved, seeds and pulp discarded, and coarsely chopped

2 avocados, pitted, peeled, and roughly chopped

small handful of fresh cilantro, chopped

Make sure you've got

1 small red onion, shredded

1 red or green chili, seeded and finely chopped

1 garlic clove, crushed (optional)

salt and pepper

juice of ¹⁄₂ lemon

❶ Mix everything, except the avocado, lemon juice, and cilantro, together. Season and chill for up to 4 hours until ready to eat.

❷ Prepare the avocado (page 74) and fold it in. Squeeze the lemon juice over, scatter the cilantro over, and serve.

per serving Energy 114 calories, protein 2.0g, carbohydrate 6.0g, fat 9.4g, saturated fat 1.1g, fiber 3.1g, added sugars none, salt 0.03g ● Super healthy; low in calories, saturated fat and salt; good source of vitamin C; counts as 2 vegetable servings on the Food Pyramid.

salsa verde (simple)

Serves 4 ● 10 minutes to prepare, plus chilling

What you need

2 scallions, shredded

1 green bell pepper, seeded and roughly chopped

2-inch piece of cucumber, unpeeled, seeded,
    and diced

1 green chili, seeded and finely chopped

finely grated zest and juice of ½ lime

small handful of fresh cilantro or mint, chopped

Make sure you've got

1 garlic clove, optional)

extra-virgin olive oil (2 tablespoons)

sugar (¼ teaspoon)

capers (1 teaspoon, rinsed and chopped)

salt and pepper

❶ Up to 4 hours ahead, mix together everything, except the herbs. Season and chill.

❷ Add the herbs and toss lightly again. Serve.

per serving
Energy 61 calories, protein 0.7g, carbohydrate 2.0g, fat 5.7g, saturated fat 0.8g, fiber 0.9g, added sugars 0.3g, salt 0.03g ● Super healthy; low in calories, fat, saturated fat and salt; good source of vitamin C.

salsa rosso (simple)

Serves 4 ● 10 minutes to prepare, plus chilling

What you need

1 small red onion, shredded

4 medium tomatoes, halved, seeds and pulp
    discarded, coarsely chopped

1 red bell pepper, seeded and coarsely chopped

8 radishes, trimmed and roughly chopped

few sprigs of purple (or green) basil

Make sure you've got

extra-virgin olive oil (2 tablespoons)

1 orange, peeled and cut into small
    pieces

salt and pepper

❶ Up to 4 hours ahead, mix together everything, except the basil. Season and chill.

❷ Toss lightly again and scatter with the basil.

per serving
Energy 97 calories, protein 1.7g, carbohydrate 9.7g, fat 6.0g, saturated fat 0.8g, fiber 2.4g, added sugars none, salt 0.03g ● Super healthy; very low in calories, saturated fat and salt; good source of vitamin C; counts as 2 vegetable servings on the Food Pyramid.

fruit fancies

Fruit is obviously one of the greatest allies of the no-cook. Good ripe fruit in season will always satisfy—and look good—with little or nothing needing to be done to it. Here, though, are some simple but effective ways with fruit that will help bring out its best qualities—a little honey here to amplify sweetness, some nuts or a little cheese there to provide a contrast in texture, alcohol and/or spices for added zing generally.

1 cherries with ricotta Put cherries and ricotta on a platter, top with some honey, and help yourselves. Grapes are also good this way—especially black seedless ones.

2 cardamom and orange-flavored fruits Slice fruits of the season and drizzle them lightly with Grand Marnier and a pinch of ground cardamom.

3 fruity yogurt Slice fresh apricots or peaches and cover with yogurt into which you have stirred a little fine-cut marmalade.

4 raspberry ripple Mix fresh or thawed raspberries with Quark or other soft, creamy low fat cheese until it is streaked and pink. Drizzle with a little honey to serve.

5 summer fruit delight Slice peaches or other summer fruits into a dish and drizzle with a little orange juice or liqueur. Crumble some amaretti cookies over and leave for a few minutes before eating.

6 **fruit salsa** Make a fruit salsa to serve with or after spicy food by chopping a small onion and adding the juice of 2 limes. Chop the flesh of a mango (or papaya, small pineapple, or 2 peaches), a small red bell pepper and plenty of cilantro. Mix, season, and splash with orange juice. You can add a finely chopped chili, if you wish.

7 **les quatre mendicants** Arrange on a plate fresh figs dusted with confectioners' sugar, walnut halves, juicy raisins, and macadamia nuts or almonds. The name refers to four monastic orders—Franciscan (gray habits), Augustinian (brown), Dominican (black), and Carmelite (white).

8 **nut-stuffed dates** Remove the pits from juicy fresh dates and replace with a mixture of chopped pistachios, pine nuts, and honey. Anoint them with rosewater just before serving.

9 **banana salad** Slice some bananas, drizzle them with lemon or lime juice and honey, and sprinkle a handful of chopped dates and walnuts over. Serve with a dollop of fromage blanc.

10 **peach-and-cherry refresher** Mix peaches and pitted cherries, and pour a little orange-flower water mixed with vodka or schnapps over.

fruit salsa

les quatre mendicants

nut-stuffed dates

banana salad

bought desserts are all well and good, but some of the most sumptuous and creative last courses of all require no more effort than melting chocolate and mixing in a few luxurious extras, or glitzing up some bought ice cream

dashing desserts

fresh raspberry truffles

Makes 20 to 24 small truffles ● 20 minutes to prepare, plus cooling and overnight chilling

This makes very soft, fresh-tasting truffles. You need a light touch—if you are the impatient sort, just don't attempt this.

What you need
5 ounces fresh or thawed frozen
    raspberries
4 ounces best-quality semisweet chocolate
4 tablespoons heavy (whipping) cream

Make sure you've got
butter (1 tablespoon)
maple syrup, honey (2 tablespoons)
unsweetened cocoa powder (2 tablespoons),
    sifted

❶ Whiz the raspberries in a food processor for 30 seconds until completely liquid. Put into a fine strainer and use a spatula or wooden spoon to squeeze the liquid through into a medium bowl, leaving the seeds behind; discard the seeds. This sounds a bother, but is actually the work of 3 to 4 minutes, and I use it as an opportunity to marvel at the stupendous bright pink raspberry color as I do so.

❷ Break the chocolate into the bowl and add the cream, butter, and syrup or honey. Heat in the microwave or over hot water, stirring frequently, until the chocolate melts and the mixture is smooth and glossy. (In my 600w microwave, it takes about 1 minute to get the mixture hot, then I stir until the chocolate is fully melted.)

❸ Stir the strained raspberry puree into the melted chocolate until completely mixed. Let cool and then refrigerate overnight, or until the mixture does not stick to your finger when pressed.

❹ Now comes the messy (fun) bit. Put the cocoa into a shallow bowl. Scoop a generous teaspoon of the mixture into your hands and roll it into a ball. Drop in the cocoa. Repeat with 4 more balls. Roll the balls about in the cocoa with a spoon and lift on to a plate lined with a piece of baking paper. Repeat with the rest of the mixture to make 20 to 24 truffles; keep chilled. Serve straight from the refrigerator, and eat within a week.

It may sound kinky, but you can use a pair of surgical gloves in Step 4 to roll and dust the truffles.

after-dinner Lamingtons

Makes 30 mini-Lamingtons (allow 1 or 2 each, but they will all get eaten regardless) ● 1 hour to prepare (put on the radio and lose yourself; best made a couple of hours ahead, although they keep for a couple of days in a tin)

Thrill an Aussie by serving chic bite-sizes of their national teatime favorite with after-dinner coffee.

What you need	Make sure you've got
14 ounces bought Madeira or pound cake, preferably square or rectangular	melted butter (3 tablespoons)
1½ cups confectioners' sugar	boiling water (3 tablespoons)
1 cup shredded coconut	unsweetened cocoa powder (1 tablespoon)
1 tablespoon raspberry jam	2 tablespoons juice and finely grated zest
1 tablespoon red-currant jelly	of ½ lemon

❶ Trim any brown parts off the cake and slice it as neatly as possible into thirty 1-inch squares. Assemble a production line: Put the cake squares on a plate, then set out a bowl for the frosting (plus a larger bowl for it to sit in), a bowl for the coconut, and 3 plates, each covered with waxed paper. You will need 2 forks for dipping in the frosting, and 2 more forks for turning the Lamingtons in the coconut.

❷ Make the chocolate frosting by mixing the 1 tablespoon of the melted butter, 1 tablespoon boiling water, the cocoa, and one-third of the confectioners' sugar. Thin to a coating consistency with another teaspoon of boiling water, if necessary.

❸ Tip a third of the coconut into the coconut bowl. One by one, put one-third of the squares in the chocolate frosting and cover all over, using the forks. Leave the excess frosting to drip off, then drop the square in the coconut. Use the other forks to roll it all over in coconut, then transfer to the paper-lined plate.

❹ The frosting will begin to set—when this happens, put boiling water in the bowl beneath the frosting, or toward the end you can add a teaspoon of boiling water.

❺ Repeat with half the remaining cake squares and raspberry frosting made in the same way as the chocolate, but replacing the cocoa with the raspberry jam and red-currant jelly. Then coat the rest of the cake squares with lemon frosting again made in the same way, replacing the cocoa with the finely grated zest and 2 tablespoons of juice from the lemon, washing the icing and dipping stations, and replenishing the coconut bowl in between.

peach tea jelly

Serves 4 to 6 ● 10 to 20 minutes to prepare (make a day ahead)

What you need
2 tablespoons orange-flavored liqueur, such as
    Curaçao or Grand Marnier
about 1½ cups Tazo peach tea (see below)
fortune cookies, to serve

Make sure you've got
sugar (4 teaspoons)
1 envelop unflavored gelatin
boiling water
juice of 1 lemon
juice of 1 orange

❶ Mix the sugar and gelatin in a cup. Pour $^{1}/_{4}$cup boiling water into a measuring jug, sprinkle the gelatin and sugar over, and stir to dissolve.

❷ When completely dissolved, add the fruit juices and liqueur and top up to about 2$^{1}/_{2}$cups with the peach tea. Stir well to make sure no solid bits of gelatin remain.

❸ Strain into wine glasses and chill to set.

❹ Serve with fortune cookies to complete the Eastern feel.

Tazo is a delicious green tea flavored with herbs and spices; you can use any other tea, but it needs to be strong and sweet ● There is a lot of nonsense talked about gelatin, but it is nothing to be scared of. Make sure it has dissolved and strain before use, in case a lump or particle has escaped your notice, and you can't go wrong.

make it your own For sheer elegance, try fresh orange jelly, made in the same way.
Dissolve the gelatin and 4 tablespoons sugar in 3 tablespoons boiling water, then add the finely grated zest of 1 orange, the juice of 4, the juice of 1 lemon, and 2 tablespoons orange-flavored liqueur. Make up to 2$^{1}/_{2}$cups, if necessary, with more juice or water. Pour into glasses (don't strain—it tastes fresher). With this formula (1 envelop unflavored powdered gelatin to 2cups liquid) you can set almost anything you can think of—coffee, smoothies, juices—you name it. Three things to remember:

❶ The mixture you're setting needs to be well sweetened.

❷ If you add liqueur or any other alcohol, the jelly does not set as firmly.

❸ If you own an elaborate jelly mold, say of Windsor Castle, and wish to use it, add 1 teaspoon extra gelatin to the mixture for a firmer set.

strawberry-misu

Serves 8 ● 20 to 30 minutes to prepare (make at least 4 hours, and up to a day, ahead)

What you need
9 ounces strawberries
9 ounces mascarpone cheese
7 ounces fromage blanc
1 small cup of espresso coffee (or 3 ounces
    strong black coffee)
5 ounces ladyfinger cookies

Make sure you've got
2 egg yolks
superfine sugar (4 tablespoons)
4 tablespoons brandy or kirsch
4 tablespoons Marsala wine
unsweetened cocoa powder for dusting

❶ Beat the egg yolks with 2 tablespoons sugar until pale and creamy—this takes a full 5 minutes by hand, 3 minutes with an electric mixer and 2 minutes in a standing mixer or food processor (if your processor is equipped with a small bowl).

❷ Mix the brandy or kirsch and the Marsala. Put the coffee in a small, wide bowl and stir in half the Marsala mix.

❸ Meanwhile, put the strawberries in a bowl with the remaining sugar and mash. Mix the mascarpone and fromage blanc, then beat in the egg yolk and the remaining Marsala mix until creamy.

❹ If you wish to make the strawberry-misu directly on a serving plate, stand the ring from an 8-inch springform cake pan in its middle; otherwise use the pan in the usual fashion. Dip the cookies very briefly in the coffee mixture (don't let them get soggy) and use to layer the bottom of the pan completely, cutting to shape as necessary.

❺ Spoon half the mascarpone mixture over to cover the cookies completely. Sift a thick dusting of cocoa over. Repeat with another layer of dunked cookies, as before, then spoon the strawberries over evenly, followed by the remaining mascarpone. Finally, dust more cocoa over and leave in the refrigerator to set. Serve cut into wedges.

If the cocoa melts into the topping, sift a fresh layer over just before serving.

make it your own This is also gorgeous with raspberries. ● If serving larger numbers, make the same size of dessert, but serve smaller portions, accompanied with extra fruit.

strawberry-misu

red fruits in a rose blanket (simple)

Serves 8 ● **10 to 20 minutes to prepare, plus leaving to stand 2 hours**

What you need
8 ounces fresh strawberries
6 ounces fresh raspberries
4 ounces red currants or black currants
1 tablespoon rosewater
1 tablespoon orange-flower water

for the rose cream
1 egg white
²/₃ cup heavy (whipping) cream
1 teaspoon rosewater
1 teaspoon orange-flower water
petals of a small well-scented rose, to strew

Make sure you've got
superfine sugar (2 tablespoons)
confectioners' sugar (2 tablespoons)

ahead
❶ Hull the strawberries and cut them in half. Pick over the raspberries and pick the currants off their stems. Arrange in a single layer in a large shallow dish, with the cut sides of the strawberries facing up. Sprinkle with the sugar and the flower waters and leave for up to 2 hours.

at the last minute
❷ Whip the egg white until it begins to stiffen and whisk in 1 tablespoon confectioners' sugar. Beat until stiff, but not dry. Using the same whisk or beaters but in another bowl, whip the cream until it is stiff, adding the remaining 1 tablespoon confectioners' sugar and the remaining 2 teaspoons flower waters. Fold in the egg white.
❸ Spoon gently over the fruits and serve scattered with rose petals.

You can crystallize rose petals by brushing them with egg white and dredging them in superfine sugar. Leave to dry on a wire rack for 4 hours. You can make these a day ahead and keep in a tin; otherwise use the petals as they are.

make it your own I love the simplicity of this dessert, but if you would like to build it into something more impressive, make individual rose meringues. Put individual meringues on plates, top with the fruit and juices, then cover generously with cream. You'll have enough for 10 to 12.

mango and lime fool (simple)

Serves 4 (easily halved or doubled) ● **15 to 25 minutes to prepare (make ahead), plus chilling**

This fool is the palest apricot color, flecked with lime zest.

What you need

1 large ripe mango (or 9 ounces prepared
    mango)

finely grated zest of 1 lime

1 tablespoon Curaçao or other orange-flavored
    liqueur

½ cup bought custard sauce

1 ¼ cups heavy (whipping) cream

Make sure you've got

superfine sugar (2 to 3 tablespoons)

ahead

❶ Puree the mango with most of the lime zest (you'll need to grate a little extra when serving) and liqueur until smooth. Add the custard sauce and sugar, and whiz the mixture again.

❷ In a big bowl, whip the cream until stiff. Pour in the mango-and-custard mixture. Use your whisk gently to combine everything until no longer streaky.

❸ Taste for sweetness—mangoes vary—and add the extra sugar if it needs it. Transfer to small glasses and chill for at least 3 hours, but preferably 24 hours.

at the last minute

❹ Grate a little extra lime zest over—for a taste of the tropics.

make it your own Add orange-flower water, instead of liqueur, for a more fragrant dessert, or try rum for something more tropical.

blackberry-mascarpone shortbread

Serves 4 (easily multiplied) ● **15 minutes to prepare**

What you need
4 ounces Scottish shortbread cookies (6 cookies)
$2/3$ cup mascarpone cheese
5 ounces fresh blackberries

Make sure you've got
butter (2 tablespoons)
honey (2 teaspoons)
confectioners' sugar, to sift over

❶ Make a shortbread crust by melting the butter in the microwave (covered with plastic wrap in case it sputters) or a pan and whizzing it with the cookies in a food processor. Tip the buttery crumbs onto a flat plate, or the rimless bottom of a tart pan, and freeze for 15 minutes. Once firm enough to handle, transfer to a serving plate and keep chilled.

❷ Just before serving, mix the mascarpone gently with the honey (far easier at room temperature), but don't overdo it or it will curdle. Spread it over the shortbread.

❸ Arrange the blackberries over the top. Dust with confectioners' sugar and serve cut in wedges.

make it your own **This is also good with strawberries, raspberries, blueberries, or a combination.**

Even easier, use one shortbread cookie $2^1/2$ to 3 inches in diameter per person. Anchor on a serving plate by dabbing a little honey in the middle. For each, mix 2 tablespoons mascarpone with $1/2$ teaspoon honey, spread on the cookie, pile on 3 ounces fruit and dust with confectioners' sugar as above.

white chocolate and summer fruit pashka

Serves 6 ● 15 to 20 minutes to prepare (make at least 2 hours, or up to a day, ahead)

What you need

5^1/$_2$ounces white chocolate, melted

^{2}/$_3$cup cottage cheese

^{1}/$_2$cup light cream cheese

^{1}/$_2$cup crème fraîche or sour cream

^{2}/$_3$cup mixed candied or dried fruits (organic
dried apricots, raisins, cherries), chopped

^{1}/$_4$cup chopped walnuts

11 ounces fresh raspberries, hulled
strawberries, or cherries

Make sure you've got

vanilla extract (1 teaspoon)

❶ Melt the white chocolate, either over a bowl of hot water or in the microwave on low for about a minute, stirring at half-time.

❷ Put the cheeses and crème fraîche in a food processor and blitz for a good minute until smooth. Add the white chocolate and vanilla.

❸ Transfer to a bowl and stir in the candied or dried fruits and the nuts. With a piece of cheesecloth about 12 inches square or a new kitchen cloth that has been rinsed and squeezed out, line a 2^1/$_2$-cup bowl or mold so the cloth hangs over the top. Spoon in the mixture and smooth the top; fold the excess cloth over the top.

❹ Leave to set in the refrigerator for at least 2 hours. When ready to serve, fold back the cloth, invert the pashka onto a dish, and remove the cloth completely. Serve the pashka in spoonfuls with the soft fruits.

In the traditional recipe, the pashka is left to drain (hence the cheesecloth). In this recipe this is not necessary, but the cloth is used to give the surface of the dessert its characteristically pretty texture.

make it your own If you have 6 ramekins, small dariole molds, or coffee cups, make individual pashkas. Line them as above, turn out into the middle of plates, and serve surrounded by the fruits.

the ultimate chocolate refrigerator cake

Cuts into 12 to 15 rich pieces ● **20 to 30 minutes to prepare**

What you need

$2/3$ cup seedless raisins

4 organic dried apricots, chopped

7 ounces semisweet chocolate (go for 70%
   cocoa solids)

$1/3$ cup sweetened chestnut puree

8 graham crackers, roughly broken

$1/2$ cup chopped toasted hazelnuts or toasted
   flaked almonds

Make sure you've got

finely grated zest of $1/2$ orange

4 tablespoons brandy

butter (1 stick, $1/4$ lb)

unsweetened cocoa powder (1 tablespoon)

confectioners' sugar for dusting

ahead

❶ Soak the raisins, apricots, and orange zest in the brandy—you can do this while you melt the chocolate, or up to a day in advance.

❷ In the microwave, or over hot water, melt the chocolate, butter, and cocoa in a large bowl. Meanwhile, line a 7-inch square pan, or an 8-x-4-inch bread pan with foil.

❸ Stir the chocolate mixture until smooth. Stir in the raisin-brandy mixture and chestnut puree, and break in the crackers roughly with the nuts. When all is glistening and well coated, transfer to your prepared pan (If using a bread pan, it will fill it to the brim.) Smooth the top carefully and put in the refrigerator.

at the last minute

❹ Cut the cake into fingers, dust with confectioners' sugar, and stack up appealingly to serve. If making in a bread pan, remove from the pan, dust with sugar and serve cut into slices.

Many recipes include an egg to stop this setting like a rock, but chestnut puree has the same effect and adds its luxurious flavor. ● **Organic dried apricots have an richer, fruitier flavor.**

make it your own You can ritz this up with chopped pistachio nuts, candied fruits of your choice, and even sliced marrons glacés. ● Instead of brandy, try kirsch, whiskey, or rum.

chocolate muffin trifles (simple)

Serves 4 ● 10 to 20 minutes to prepare

What you need

3 chocolate muffins

$^2/_3$cup whipping cream

5 tablespoons Tia Maria or amaretto, plus
    more for sprinkling

9ounces mascarpone cheese

Make sure you've got

semisweet chocolate (5ounces), melted

ahead

❶ Have ready 4 large glasses. Crumble the muffins lightly into a bowl. Melt the chocolate over hot water or in the microwave and leave to cool slightly.

❷ Whip the cream until stiff, adding the 5tablespoons liqueur toward the end. If using an electric mixer, use it to beat the mascarpone until soft. Now combine the cream and mascarpone, using the whisk in a cutting action, or the beaters of the electric mixer, not actually turning.

❸ Pour the cooled chocolate over and lightly fold together until rippled—stop before you think you're done, as you want a strong effect.

❹ Divide half the muffin crumble between the glasses. Sprinkle each lightly with some of the liqueur.

❺ Spoon or pour half the chocolate mixture over. Then repeat the layers.

make it your own Use a potato peeler to flick over chocolate curls.

kirsch ice-cream cake (simple)

Serves 6 to 8 ● 10 to 20 minutes to prepare, plus freezing time

This recipe is based on a dessert created many years ago by a London hotel in honor of a long-forgotten royal wedding. It is unusual and sophisticated.

What you need

2 cups heavy (whipping) cream, or a mixture
   of heavy cream and crème fraîche or
   sour cream

3 tablespoons kirsch or vodka

6 to 8 bought meringues (about 3 ounces),
   broken up

Make sure you've got

finely grated zest of 1 lemon

4 slices of candied ginger, finely chopped

ahead

❶ Line a shallow round 7-inch cake pan with plastic wrap.

❷ Whip the cream until just stiff. Fold in the remaining ingredients, including the meringues (it's tidiest to break them up while still in the wrapper—aim for pieces no bigger than a walnut). Pile into the pan and smooth the top.

❸ Freeze for at least 4 hours.

at the last minute

❹ About 10 minutes before serving, turn out onto a serving plate, remove the plastic wrap, and serve cut in wedges.

This is a very rich and exciting dessert, best served with sharp fruits such as Cape gooseberry, strawberries or raspberries, or pineapple or orange in winter. Alternatively, serve with a fruit coulis.

frozen assets

Test whether ice cream is too hard or ready to serve with a thin skewer. About 15 to 30 minutes in the refrigerator gives most ices time to soften; this is far easier than doing battle with a bricklike block of ice and bending your best spoon into the bargain. If you're in a hurry, microwave in bursts.

1 instant warm chocolate sauce Heat $^2/_3$cup light cream with 1 tablespoon sugar and a knob of butter until boiling. Whiz 4ounces semisweet chocolate in a processor and pour in the hot cream. Process until smooth. Add a few drops of vanilla extract, brandy, or rum. Great with vanilla, butterscotch, or chocolate ice cream.

2 hot espresso sauce Make $^3/_4$cup very strong coffee. While still very hot, whisk in 7ounces semisweet chocolate, finely chopped, and 4 tablespoons ($^1/_2$ stick) butter. Great with coffee, chocolate, or vanilla ice cream.

3 ice-cream pie Make the crumb crust on page 153 and freeze it in its pan. Allow $1^1/_2$ to 2pints ice cream to soften just enough to make it easy to spoon, and pack half into the crust. Top the layer of ice cream with a few handfuls of sliced Mars Bars, then spread the rest of the ice cream over. Freeze again and top with more Mars Bars or chocolate nuts to serve.

4 butterscotch ripple ice cream Stir dulce de leche into soft vanilla ice cream until streaky. Serve at once with a warm or hot sauce. You can warm dulce de leche (South American sweetened thickened milk) in the microwave to make an instant butterscotch sauce.

5 ice-cream surprise By the same principle, you can stir any or several of the following into softened vanilla ice cream: chocolate espresso beans, chopped mint chocolate, chopped Toblerone, chopped chocolate cookies, chopped marshmallows, M&Ms (though the color runs a bit alarmingly). If you want to do this ahead, go for softer scoop ice cream, and don't let it melt too far before refreezing.

6 ice-cream sandwiches Make ice cream sandwiches by freezing 2 large thin cookies per person. When frozen, sandwich with just-softened ice cream, press chopped chocolate or nuts round the side, and refreeze again until firm, wrapping each sandwich tightly in plastic wrap. This is a great individual dessert to keep for when you deserve a treat.

7 sprinkle toppings Add some sparkle with ice-cream sprinkles. After scooping, sprinkle with chocolate nuts and raisins, jelly beans, crushed cookies, miniature marshmallows, or chopped chocolates.

8 Italian affogato For Italian affogato, put a scoop of vanilla ice cream in a heatproof dish or glass and pour over a small amount of very strong hot espresso.

9 fruit coulis Make raspberry, strawberry, or blueberry coulis by blending 9 ounces fresh or thawed berries with the juice of $1/2$ lemon. If using raspberries, press through a strainer with a spatula or wooden spoon, frequently scraping the underside, which speeds things up. Stir in sugar to taste—about 3 tablespoons. Strawberry coulis can be a bit pale, so add a handful of raspberries if you wish, plus extra lemon juice to sharpen. Blueberry coulis may start to set, so thin with water, if necessary. Serve with fruit ice creams or vanilla.

10 Grand Marnier fruits Keep a jar to drizzle over vanilla ice cream. Chop a mixture of candied and dried fruits and spices—cherries, root ginger, mixed peel, raisins, dried apricots (good for using up the ends of packages)—and put in a jar. Cover with Grand Marnier, Cointreau, or brandy and leave in the refrigerator for at least a week and up to 2 months. (Also great drizzled between layers of a bread-and-butter pudding.)

fruit coulis

ice-cream sandwiches

sprinkle toppings

Italian affogato

mocha hedgehog (simple)

Serves 6 ● 15 to 25 minutes to prepare (make a day in advance or freeze, up to the end of Step 3)

This is grand and impressive, but astonishingly simple to make.

What you need

3/4 cup very finely ground blanched almonds

4 ounces Rich Tea or other plain vanilla
    cookies (about 15 cookies)

Make sure you've got

strong black coffee (7 ounces)

unsalted butter (6 tablespoons)

superfine sugar (1 tablespoon)

for the finishing touch

1/2 cup whole toasted almonds, or 1/4 cup
    toasted slivered almonds

2/3 cup double cream

coffee-flavored liqueur (1 tablespoon)

ahead

❶ Make the coffee (the easiest way is to filter it into a large measuring jug) and, while still hot, stir in the butter and sugar. Stir until the butter melts, then stir in the ground almonds. Break in the cookies and leave for about 10 minutes until the sauce is beginning to thicken.
❷ Line a 2 1/2-cup bowl with plastic wrap. Pour in the cookies mixture and smooth the top. Refrigerate overnight. If using whole toasted almonds, split them in half down the middle.

shortly before serving

❸ Whip the cream until stiff and, as it thickens, beat in the liqueur until the cream is stiff. Unmold the cake onto a plate, peel off the plastic wrap, and spoon the cream over. Stick the nuts all over, hedgehog-fashion.

cantuccini log (simple)

Serves 6 ● **20 to 30 minutes to prepare, plus time to chill**

This is a grownup variation of the chocolate-chip log many of us made as children.

What you need

5 ounces cantuccini (Italian almond cookies)
cookies (20 small cookies)

1 cup heavy (whipping) cream

chocolate to grate on top

Make sure you've got

finely grated zest and juice of 1 orange

orange-flavored liqueur (2 tablespoons)

ground allspice ($\frac{1}{2}$ teaspoon)

ahead

❶ Practice the shape by arranging a row of 10 cantuccini biscuits upright with another 10 on top of them in a second layer. Choose your serving plate.

❷ Beat the orange zest and juice with half the liqueur. Whip the cream with the allspice and remaining liqueur until soft peaks form.

❸ Dip a cookie first in the orange mixture, then put a spoonful of cream on top and stand the cookie as it was first time around. Continue until you have your bottom layer. Spoon a little cream on top, then continue with second layer.

❹ If you have any orange mixture left, fold it into remaining cream, then spread the cream over the "log" and drag a fork across to make an attractive pattern.

❺ Refrigerate for a couple of hours or overnight.

at the last minute

❻ Sprinkle with grated chocolate. Serve cut in slices.

Make it your own You can use flavored or chocolate-chip cantuccini. ● You can use ground cinnamon or nutmeg instead of the allspice if that's what you have.

glossy choc-peanut butter cheesecake

Serves 8 ● 20 to 30 minutes to prepare (make ahead)

If you're feeling indulgent, you may as well do the job properly. This cheesecake is the dessert equivalent of Reese's Pieces—only it's much nicer.

What you need for the crust

7 ounces graham crackers (about 14), put in a bag and finely crushed with a rolling pin

for the filling

1 cup plus 2 tablespoons cream cheese

1/2 cup peanut butter (smooth or chunky, as you wish)

1 1/4 cups heavy (whipping) cream

for the glossy topping

2 ounces semisweet chocolate, broken into pieces

Make sure you've got

butter (1 stick, 1/4 lb), melted

maple syrup (2 tablespoons)

super fine sugar (1/4 cup)

confectioners' sugar (1/4 cup)

❶ Line an 8-inch springform cake pan with waxed paper. Put three-quarters of the butter and the syrup in a medium bowl and melt in the microwave or over hot water. Stir in the crackers. Turn into the pan and, using your hands, press all over the bottom and slightly up the side. Refrigerate while you make the filling.

❷ Put the cream cheese, peanut butter, and sugar in a food processor and whiz—the mixture will be heavy and sticky. Pour 3/4 cup of the cream into the peanut-butter mixture and process, scraping down the side as necessary. Spoon into the crust, smoothing the top carefully with a spatula to get it dead level.

❸ Put the remaining cream, butter, chocolate, and confectioners' sugar in a bowl and melt in the microwave or over hot water. Whisk until smooth and glossy. Pour on top of the peanut-butter filling and chill for at least an hour or overnight.

bitter-sweet chocolate torte

Serves 8 to 10 ● **30 to 40 minutes to prepare (make at least 4 hours ahead)**

This may look complex, but it's actually quite easy, intensely chocolaty, and wonderfully alcoholic.

For the crumb crust
2 ounces semisweet chocolate
6 ounces graham crackers (about 12 crackers)

For the bittersweet chocolate filling
5 ounces bittersweet chocolate

For the topping
1¼ cups heavy (whipping) cream
unsweetened cocoa powder or a few chocolate
   coffeebeans

Make sure you've got
unsweetened cocoa powder (2 tablespoons)
butter (½ stick, 4 tablespoons)
sugar (6 tablespoons)
4 tablespoons freshly brewed extra-strong
   espresso or filter coffee
4 eggs, separated
vanilla extract (1 teaspoon)
brandy (4 tablespoons)

ahead

❶ Place the ring from an 8-inch springform cake pan upside down on a serving plate and line the edge with waxed paper. To make the crust, melt the chocolate with the cocoa powder and butter in a large bowl in a microwave or over hot water. Blitz the crackers and 2 tablespoons sugar in a food processor until soft and crumbly—but don't continue until they turn to sand. Stir into the melted chocolate mixture, then pile into the lined pan. Use a spoon and your fingers to press the crumbs lightly up the side, then over the bottom. You will need an interior depth of at least 1½-inches. Do not make the top too straight—a thinner and wavier edge is more attractive, while a straight one can vanish to nothing—and avoid a thick heel of crumbs in the corner. Put in the refrigerator to chill while you make the mousse filling.

❷ Make the filling: Melt the chocolate in the coffee in a microwave or over hot water. Meanwhile, beat the egg yolks with the vanilla. Stir in the chocolate and, when smooth, the brandy.

❸ Beat 3 of the egg whites until almost stiff, then start beating in 3 tablespoons of sugar. Continue until the mixture forms peaks when you lift the beaters, and the peaks fall, rather than stay upright. Fold into the chocolate mixture, then transfer to the chilled crust. Chill for at least 4 hours, or overnight.

to finish

❹ Remove the springform ring and lining paper. Softly whip the cream with 1 tablespoon sugar until just stiffening, and billow over the filling. Dust with cocoa powder or decorate with chocolate coffeebeans to serve.

For the full-on chocolate effect, use 70% cocoa solids chocolate throughout.

make it your own You can flavor this torte with whiskey or a liqueur, rather than brandy. Bourbon or rum work beautifully, or Amaretto, or the hazelnut-flavored Frangelico. ● Decorate it in your own style. Simply grate chocolate, or make chocolate curls. If using amaretto liqueur in the torte, go for toasted almonds or chocolate almonds; if Frangelico, go for hazelnuts. ● For an extra-bouffant topping, whisk a large egg white with 1 tablespoon sugar to the soft peak stage and fold into the cream.

bittersweet chocolate torte

the no-cook pantry, etc.

The basics the no-cook should have in stock
(the "Make sure you've gots")

anchovy fillets
balsamic vinegar
*bananas
brandy
*bread (white)
capers
caraway seeds
cayenne
*chilies (fresh)
chutney
cider vinegar
coriander (ground)
cornichons
quick-cooking couscous
cumin
curry paste
*eggs
extra-virgin olive oil
fish sauce (nam pla)
*garlic
unflavored powdered gelatin
golden raisins or seedless
   raisins
good-quality bouillon granules
green onions
harissa paste
hoisin sauce
honey
horseradish
horseradish sauce
Japanese rice wine
maple syrup
marsala
mayonnaise

*milk
mustard (Dijon)
mustard (wholegrain)
nutmeg
olive oil
olives
*onions (yellow and red)
*oranges
oregano (dried)
paprika
peanut butter
pesto sauce
pine nuts
rice noodles (instant)
rice wine vinegar
*root ginger
rosewater
salt and freshly ground black
   pepper
sesame oil (toasted)
sherry (dry)
sherry vinegar
soy sauce
sugar, white
sugar, brown
sun-dried tomatoes (in oil)
sunflower oil
sunflower oil (toasted)
Tabasco sauce
Thai sweet chili sauce
tomato catsup
tomato paste or sun-dried
   tomato paste
tuna (canned)
vermicelli
walnut oil
white-wine vinegar
Worcestershire sauce

Other ingredients invaluable to the no-cook
(many of these are already in the lists at the front of the book)

argan oil
arugula
avruga (herring) caviar
basil
butter (unsalted)
cannellini beans (canned)
celery
chervil
chilies (crushed)
chives
cilantro (fresh leaves)
cinnamon (ground)
crème fraîche
cucumber
custard sauce
fava beans (young)
feta in oil
fromage blanc
garbanzo beans (canned)
goat cheese
ice cream
limes
mascarpone cheese
paprika
parsley
peas
poppy seeds
shrimp
smoked salmon
smoked paprika
tarragon
tomatoes
watercress

* non-pantry item, such as one for the refrigerator or freezer

index

acknowledgements

My thanks to everyone who has inspired the recipes in this book, especially Henrietta Green for her generous sharing of ideas and expertise.

Since my schooldays, my sounding board on all matters culinary has been Stephen Mudge, now based in Paris. I would like to thank him for his benign influence over the years I have been cooking, and his suggestions for this book.

The team at BBC Good Food is a daily inspiration to work with, and I never stop learning from them—thanks especially to Mary Cadogan, Angela Nilsen, Sara Buenfeld, Barney Desmazery, and Jeni Wright, as well as the unflappable Sarah Astell and nutritionist Dr Wendy Doyle, who prepared the nutritional analyses for my healthy eating chapter.

The philosophy of this book is that ingredients are everything: I would like to thank Thane Prince for opening my eyes to this at her Aldeburgh Cookery School, in Suffolk, England, and Francesca Fabbri, who enlightened me on bruschetta and crostini.

At Quadrille Publishing, my thanks go to Alison Cathie, Jane O'Shea, Lewis Esson, and Mary Evans for their talent and professionalism. Also to Jason Lowe and Jane Suthering for their mouthwatering photographs.

Finally, for support and encouragement during the arduous weeks of recipe development and testing, Peter Steggall, Pat and Patsy Murrin, and Andrew Leonard.